# The Business Side of General Dental Practice

## MAKING SENSE OF

# Dental

# Practice

# Finance

**Mervyn J Bright,** F.C.A., A.T.I.I., Chartered Accountant
and
**Sau-Kee Li,** A.T.T., Tax Manager

*Series Editor:* Raj Rattan, B.D.S., D.G.D.P. (UK), part-time General Dental
Practitioner; Vocational Training Adviser (N.E. Thames region) to
B.P.M.F., University of London; Dental Adviser Bromley Health;
part-time Dento-Legal Adviser, Dental Protection Ltd.; author and Adviser
to *The Dentist* magazine; Regional Adviser to BUPA DentalCover.

RADCLIFFE MEDICAL PRESS
Oxford and New York

British Library Cataloguing in Publication Data
A catalogue record for this book is available from the British Library

ISBN 185775 065 9

Typeset by AMA Graphics Limited
Printed and bound in Great Britain by
Biddles Ltd, Guildford and King's Lynn

# Contents

# Preface

Dental surgeons are notoriously disorganized when it comes to finance, and in recent years there has been an escalation in the numbers finding themselves in difficulty with Inland Revenue investigations and, in extreme cases, facing insolvency, something which is new to the profession.

Although the dental schools produce excellent clinicians, they do not see it as part of their function to train graduates for entry into the business world and, like it or not, a dental practice is a business, which has to compete in the harsh commercial world to achieve profitability.

Before 1991 Dental Protection ran a series of one-day seminars at a number of dental schools under the title 'And Now To Practice', which were designed to give undergraduates in their last few months at university a taste of what was yet to come. The lecturers came from the legal profession, accountancy, insurance, the GDC and from the Board itself. Sadly, the combined effects of the recession and lack of enthusiasm by the students themselves, something that they no doubt will come to regret when they are actually faced with the reality of general practice, brought the courses to an end, leaving undergraduates with a dearth of knowledge on the business side of dentistry.

It was whilst considering how we might fill the gap in literature on this topic that we received an approach from Radcliffe Medical Press to produce this work and we welcomed the invitation.

We hope that not only will this book fill the gap for the GDP and the potential practitioner, but will also prove of benefit to some of our own colleagues who have little practical experience of dental accounting and the peculiarities of the profession.

We would like to express our appreciation to the many people who have assisted us with information, but would particularly wish to mention Mr Lynn Walters of Dental Protection Ltd.

Mervyn Bright
Sau-Kee Li
*Poole, Dorset*
*July, 1994.*

# The dental profession

Prior to 1921 the dental profession was not formally organized and, whilst there were training courses, many practitioners had learned their trade as 'apprentices' and lacked theoretical or medical education. Attempts to establish a dental register were unsuccessful until the Dentists Act (1921), when, unfortunately, it was necessary to accept on the Register many practitioners with dubious qualifications. Approaching 7000 dentists found credibility by this means, although all have now left the Register. It was also necessary to authorize a number of limited companies onto the Register, and today 28 of these remain, although it is not possible for any new companies to be set up for the purpose of practising dentistry.

## The general dental council

The General Dental Council (GDC) is a statutory body comprising a President and 49 members. It is charged with the responsibility under the Dentists Act (1984) of supervising education and examination of dental undergraduates and dental auxiliaries in the UK. It maintains a Register of those persons entitled to practise dentistry and approves such overseas courses as are acceptable for inclusion on the Register. Every dental surgeon in the UK is subject to the professional standards and disciplinary procedures prescribed by the GDC, which has the power to suspend or erase names from the Register in appropriate cases.

On 1 January 1993 there were 27,068 dentists on the Register, of which 7145 (26.4%) were women, 137 (0.5%) EU nationals, 1160 (4.3%) commonwealth nationals and 931 (3.4%) foreign graduates. The breakdown of this figure between the dental schools is shown in Figure 1.1.

The number of new graduates has shown a fairly steady growth since 1948 (Figure 1.2) and the number of practitioners on the Register, although somewhat erratic, has shown a similar growth trend over the same period (Figure 1.3).

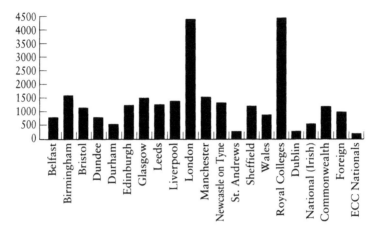

**Figure 1.1** Number of Graduates

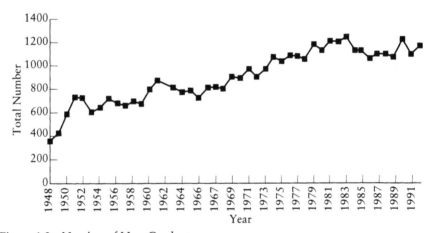

**Figure 1.2** Number of New Graduates

## The dentist's career

On graduating, and after enrolment on the Dentists' Register, the new dental surgeon will have a number of options:

1  To take up a hospital or Community Health Service appointment as an employee.
2  To join the Armed Services (where the dental course was sponsored by the Services there will probably be an obligation to do so for a specified time).
3  To enter the academic world or take up appointment in an advisory capacity using dental skills.

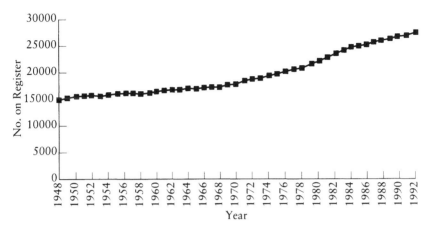

**Figure 1.3** Number of Graduates on Register

4 To enter professional practice, either as a general dental practitioner (GDP) or as a specialist.

Statistics demonstrating how the 27,068 registered dental practitioners are currently employed are difficult to come by, especially as some dentists will work in more than one category. However, it would seem that about 83% are in general practice.

From 1 October 1993 every new graduate will be required to undergo a period of vocational training before they are eligible to practise in the general dental services (GDS) as an independent contractor and obtain an FHSA list number. It is estimated that more than 50% of dentists in general practice work as associates and that there are approximately 600–650 vocational trainees at any time.

## The National Health Service

Before the National Health Services Act (1946) introduced the concept of free health services, dental treatment was funded privately and, inevitably, the standard of dental health was low. In the early days of the health service, treatment was very much oriented towards extractions, but with the passage of time, public awareness of dental hygiene, and more advanced treatment methods, there has been a change of emphasis to preventive treatment as opposed to simply remedial work. It is a far cry from the days when it was customary to give young women a full clearance and dentures as a wedding present.

Since 1946 the Secretary of State for Social Services has been charged with the responsibility of establishing a comprehensive health service, to include dental treatment. This task was delegated to the Family Practitioner Committees (now known as the Family Health Service Authorities (FHSAs)) in England and Wales and to the Health Boards in Scotland and Ireland. These bodies deal with the day-to-day administration, including the local register of NHS dentists and dealing with complaints from the general public. The ultimate control over matters of professional judgement, such as giving prior approval to estimates or passing the dentists' claims for payment, lies with the Dental Practice Board.

Over recent years there have been many changes affecting dentistry, in particular the amount which the patient is required to pay towards the cost of dental treatment. However, the greatest change took place in October 1990, with the introduction of the New Contract negotiated between the British Dental Association and the Secretary of State.

Prior to the New Contract the dentist had been remunerated on an item of service basis alone, with the only wholly free treatment being provided for people receiving certain benefits from the DHSS, pregnant or nursing mothers, students (full time) aged 19 years or less and children up to the age of 18 years. Under the New Contract a capitation payment (following an entry payment) was introduced for children. This was calculated on a sliding scale according to age, in return for which the practitioner is required to keep the child dentally fit. The range of entry payment is from £27 to £83; the capitation fee is from 45p per month for a child of 2 years up to £3.60 per month at age 17. A continuing care payment was introduced for adults. This provided a monthly payment (between 24p and 40p) over a two-year period, which was designed to represent about 20% of the dentists' total pay, the remainder coming from an item of service payment as before, although the fee scale has changed. Free treatment is available to exempt groups as before.

Whereas the dentist had previously been required to ensure that the patient was *dentally fit* at the end of a course of treatment, the New Contract demands that the patient be maintained as *orally healthy* and, for the first time, the relationship between dentist and patient was not confined to the course of treatment but was on a continuing basis.

Although supporters of the contract saw this as providing a more regular and stable monthly income, which would ease cash flow problems, a far greater number of practitioners feared it would erode both their working conditions and incomes. It became clear that a number were giving serious consideration to opting out of the NHS and confining themselves to private work, previously representing about 12% of the gross fee income in an average mixed NHS/private practice.

In the event, after a period of cash flow difficulty, dentists found their incomes increasing substantially and, indeed, this was noted by the Secretary of State for Health who, in 1992, cut dentists' pay by 7% to compensate for the unexpectedly high growth in earnings.

This was the catalyst for the movement from NHS to private dentistry, and in some areas of the country FHSAs have been forced to offer financial incentives to encourage practitioners to set up NHS facilities. These incentives may take the form of a grant or interest-free loan. In the absence of such initiatives, the FHSA would find itself unable to fulfil its obligations under the National Health Service Act (1946) for provision of dental services.

## Private dental health schemes

Over the years there have been several attempts to establish private dental health insurance schemes, but these have not been successful. The main problem has been that whereas in general medicine it is relatively straightforward to distinguish between essential and desirable treatment, this has not been the case in dentistry, with the result that insurance companies found themselves faced with claims for what could be considered to be more cosmetic than necessary treatment.

With the escalation of dental practices leaving the NHS system, a number of dental health schemes were established eg Denplan/PPP and BUPA DentalCover. Essentially these were a means by which patients could make a monthly payment in return for the dentist agreeing to provide private treatment to keep them dentally fit. Such schemes ensure that the practitioner has a guaranteed, regular monthly income, the pressure of NHS work is removed, and patients can be given more time and better materials than the NHS scale of fees permitted.

Even so, the general public has been slow to respond and companies offering these schemes have inevitably sustained heavy losses in the initial years. Few have had the resources to survive and indeed, few have been able to compete with Denplan Ltd, which set up such a scheme on a nationwide basis in 1987. In some cases practitioners have observed the simplicity of the Denplan scheme and have established similar systems, without some of the frills, through their own practices.

## Dentists' pay under the NHS

The procedure to determine dentists' pay under the NHS has not changed materially in spite of the New Contract.

Initially the Review Body on Doctors' and Dentists' Remuneration will recommend a target average net income for dentists (TANI). The Dental Rates Study Group (DRSG) will then fix the target average gross income (TAGI), which is TANI plus the anticipated level of practice expenses for the next year, based on information gleaned from the Inland Revenue on expenses in past years (Figure 1.4).

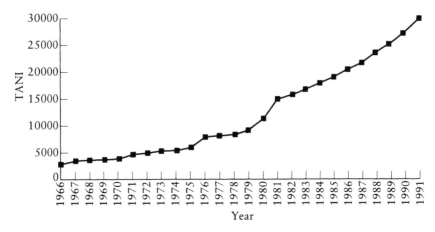

**Figure 1.4**　Target Average Net Income (TANI)

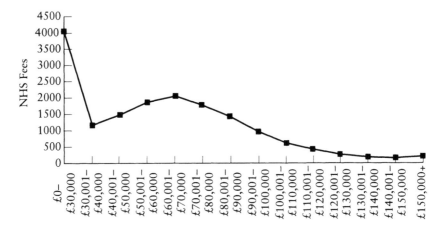

**Figure 1.5**　GDP Annual NHS Earnings Pattern

Sources of information used by the Review Body include.

1　Written evidence from the BDA and Health Departments.
2　Jointly agreed statistical data.
3　Independent evidence, eg the result of surveys.
4　Inland Revenue enquiries into GDP expenses.

Efforts are then made to ensure that a scale of fees is constructed that reflects materials and laboratory charges as well as the expected time needed to complete a procedure. It is sometimes necessary to make adjustments from year to year to compensate for changes in practice expenses.

The system is necessarily based on averages, which means that some practitioners will earn more and some less than TANI. Figure 1.5 shows that the majority of practitioners earned gross NHS fees of between £40,000 and £100,000 in 1992. In fact, 32% grossed below £40,000 and 10% above £100,000.

Dentists receive their NHS income in three parts. The patient will pay 80% of the total NHS fee (unless they fall into one of the exemption categories) and it is the practitioner's responsibility to collect this. The balance of the item of service element is paid by the DPB. The third portion is the child entry or capitation payment and the continuing care payment, both of which are paid by the DPB.

## Payments made by the DPB

1   Entry payment to achieve dental fitness and a monthly capitation payment (children only).
2   Continuing care payments and item of service payments (adults only).
3   Postgraduate education allowance (restricted to a claim for two sessions per year) for approved courses.
4   Seniority allowance.
5   Vocational training grant and reimbursement of vocational trainee salary.
6   Rates reimbursement.
7   Specific grants, eg for EDI.

The DPB has to give prior approval to courses of treatment which exceed £200. This will entail examining radiographs, study casts and the dentist's report. In some instances, prior approval for particular treatment is imposed on a practitioner for a specified period of time as a disciplinary measure if a practitioner has been found in breach of his/her Terms of Service by the FHSA.

# The future

At the time of writing the future of the organization and management of the General Dental Services remains uncertain despite the publication of a government Green Paper 'Improving NHS Dentistry', which focuses on optimizing available resources, with the aim of providing a comprehensive NHS dental service which meets today's needs and which is also acceptable to the profession.

This document has been widely circulated and opinions are being sought from the profession and its representatives. It is envisaged that there will be radical changes to the system to overcome the deficiencies in the present system of remuneration, as highlighted in the Bloomfield Report which was published in January 1993 and confirmed by the Health Select Committee's report, which was published in June of the same year. It is likely that the purchaser-provider model, now well established in health-care, will be a key issue in the debate.

Certainly, there is an upward trend in private dental care and all the evidence suggests that is likely to continue.

# 2

# Vocational trainees, assistants and associates

## The vocational trainee

As from 1 October 1993 all new graduates will be required to undergo a period as a vocational trainee in a training practice. The object is to give the newly qualified dentist an opportunity to acclimatize to the rigours of general practice after the sheltered surroundings of dental school. The trainee receives a salary, currently 50% of TANI, which is paid by the trainer who can then reclaim it via the Dental Practice Board. The monies for the salary derive from the GDS pool.

The training practice is selected after inspection of its facilities and interview of the GDP(s) to ensure that they have the requisite qualifications and can offer suitable training facilities. The vocational trainee is a fully qualified dental surgeon working under the guidance of a more experienced and professionally mature colleague (the trainer).

The training practice is given a training grant equivalent at present to 15% of the target average net income (TANI), and retains all fee income generated by the trainee. In return the training practice is required to ensure that the vocational trainee is given proper training facilities, including the opportunity to attend a vocational trainee course of 30 study days spread over three 10-week terms. The vocational trainee is also entitled to four weeks annual paid holiday and will work a maximum of 35 hours each week, except during term time when this will be reduced to 28 hours.

Competition for placement in training practices in some areas has been very high, and this may necessitate trainees moving outside the area of their choice.

# The assistant

Whilst at one time it was commonplace to find a dentist being employed as an assistant on a salary and working on the principal's FHSA number, today it is less common. The problem is that the assistant is an employee and the principal is vicariously liable for his/her acts and omissions as an employer, but wholly responsible as far as NHS contractual obligations to the FHSA are concerned. In matters of professional misconduct involving the GDC, the assistant is answerable to the GDC but the principal may also be involved if it was demonstrated that both parties were implicated in the original offence. Vocational trainees have assistant status.

# The locum

Dentists in group practices will often be able to leave the care of their patients with a partner when they are on holiday or on extended sick leave, but this is not possible for a single-handed practitioner. In such cases it is usual to appoint a locum: a qualified dentist who chooses to work on a self-employed basis for short periods in different practices. Usually, the locum will be paid on the day-book basis, which means that they are paid for the work actually carried out during the period, and so do not have to wait for the DPB to process claim forms. The major problem with a locum is that they will have been paid on completion of the task, irrespective of any problems that later come to light, which may then result in a withholding from the DPB.

# The associate

The 'associate' is a dentist, usually between the vocational trainee stage and setting up in practice on their own account as a principal; in law, associates are self-employed independent contractors.

The concept of an 'associate' is unique to the dental profession and came into existence through the NHS method of payment. The average earnings of a dental practitioner were determined by the amount paid by reference to their FHSA number; there was no way of distinguishing between the sole practitioner or the GDP employing several assistants. As a result, the average earnings appeared higher than was the case in reality. The profession overcame this by creating the associate, who works under their own FHSA number with patients and facilities provided by the principal.

In return, the associate will pay the principal a proportion of their gross fee earnings, but does not acquire any rights over the goodwill or other assets of the practice.

## Method of payment

The associate can be remunerated in a number of ways:

1   The associate will assign their fee income to the principal (ie the DPB is directed to make payment to the GDP's bank) and the principal will also collect the patients' contributions. The associate is paid their share when the DPB makes the bank transfer.
2   The associate collects the payments from the DPB and contributions from their own patients, and will then pay the principal the agreed proportion.

There are difficulties inherent in both methods. In the first, a new problem has emerged as a result of the recent recession. Where the principal has encountered financial difficulties and been adjudicated bankrupt, the associate has often been found to be unable to obtain payment from the Trustee in Bankruptcy because it is claimed he is a subcontractor, ranking *pari passu* with the unsecured creditors rather than as a preferential claimant for salary, because associates are not employees. There is also the risk that, in the event of a dispute, the associate may revoke the fee assignment by writing to the DPB.

In the second case, some principals have had associates refusing to meet their obligations, and have been forced to issue legal proceedings to recover the funds.

Thankfully, these problems are infrequent, but they are nevertheless serious when they do occur. By far the best solution is for the first course to be adopted but for the principal to receive the associate's remuneration into a separate bank account designated as 'Associate's Monies'. From here the payment can be split between the parties as agreed, without risk of any third party claiming a right set-off in respect of the funds. It would also keep this money out of the hands of a Trustee in Bankruptcy. As a precaution the bank should be made aware of the fact that the 'Associates Monies' account is not the property of the principal.

More recently, another payment for associates has emerged; a sort of 'rent' for use of the surgery facilities and a supply of the patients. This has the advantage of ensuring that the principal is aware of their income and will be entitled to receive it irrespective of the associate's earnings. However, unless the 'rent' is fixed at a fair level for both parties, there can be a measure of jealously if the associate is able to gross fees likely to give a substantial profit on outgoings. If this method is adopted, then it is essential for both parties to agree on a fair 'rent' from the outset and to adhere to it and also to agree how often it should be reviewed.

Payment on the day-book basis is not common and is certainly not recommended except perhaps in the early stages when delays in payment from the DPB can create short-term cash flow difficulties.

## Amount of contribution

Traditionally, associates have been paid 50% of their gross fee income after deduction of laboratory fees. There may be additional deductions for outstanding debts and hygienists' salaries.

There has been a recent trend towards the sliding scale dependent on the associate's monthly gross fee income. This means that the associate will contribute a greater portion of their fees when earnings are low but will retain more as the fees increase. This arrangement is designed to protect the principal against subsidising associates costs if the associate fails to meet their share of the practice costs.

Yet another problem is the fact that, with the percentage contribution, the principal will be adversely affected when the associate is on holiday, on courses or absent through illness. The costs continue whilst the fee income, and consequently the contribution, has ceased. This can be overcome by introducing a minimum payment and ensuring that the associate takes out an insurance policy to cover the expense in case of prolonged illness.

It is, of course, possible to have an 'expense-sharing' associate, rather like the 'expense sharing' partner (*see* Chapter 13), although not owning any part of the practice.

The associate is usually given a summary showing how their earnings are calculated. It would also be helpful for the associate to have a copy of the front page of his NHS Schedule, whilst the principal ought to retain a copy of the payslip with the original copy of the Schedule and the backing sheets.

*Associate's pay slip*

Gross fee income

| | |
|---|---|
| National Health | £6,200 |
| Private | £1,400 |
| Total gross | £7,600 |

Deductions

| | |
|---|---|
| Laboratory fees | £1,450 |
| Bad debts | £250 |
| Total deductions | £1,700 |
| | £5,900 |
| 50% (agreed percentage) | £2,850 |
| Superannuation | £250 |
| Net pay cheque (before tax) | £2,600 |

## Associateship agreement

All too often the parties are so keen to establish a principal/associate relationship that they fail to ensure that they are properly protected by a formal agreement. This can have serious consequences, particularly where the parties disagree.

No associate should take up an appointment until they have negotiated and entered into a written agreement with the proposed principal setting out the terms and conditions agreed. It is seldom possible to put such an agreement into place once the arrangement has begun, and certainly not once a dispute has arisen.

The agreement should not be negotiated until the prospective associate has inspected the practice, preferably during working hours when they can meet the staff and see how the surgeries operate. The associate should also be quite clear as to the facilities and the patient list size and should glance at the appointment book to make sure that there is an adequate demand for professional services. It is also prudent to enquire why the previous associate left.

Typical provisions in an associate agreement will be:

1   The identification of the parties.
2   The date of commencement and duration of the arrangement.
3   Provisions for its termination on either side.
4   A clear and concise indication of the terms of the agreement, ie how the gross fees will be apportioned and what expenses are to be deducted.
5   An indication of how the associate will fare in the early days of the arrangement, ie details of any advances or other adjustments between day-book earnings and fees actually received.
6   Details of the arrangement for payment of fees including any arrears at the termination of the agreement.
7   Details of any 'barring out' clause.
8   Details of any legal obligations imposed on the associate.
9   A requirement that the associate is on the Dentists Register and that they will maintain membership of one of the protection societies.

### 'Barring out' clause

Any principal will presumably wish to ensure that an associate, having built up a reputation, will not leave and establish a competitive practice nearby, which could result in loss of goodwill and patients. This can be achieved by the inclusion of a 'barring out' clause in the associate agreement. However, it is not possible to include such a clause once the arrangement is in force, unless the associate is in agreement. Without such a clause the associate is free to practise where they wish and the principal has no redress. However, it should be remembered that even a barring out clause can be challenged in court if it is deemed to be unreasonable. In an urban area the distance and time will be considerably less than in a rural community.

It is always sensible to seek legal advice or advice from one of the professional protection societies when drawing up an associateship agreement. There are four specimen agreements in the BDA booklet *Practising together*.

## Accounting records

The associate will need to maintain accounting records showing details of income and expenditure. However, as their affairs will usually be comparatively straightforward, the records can be quite simple.

A typical account book for an associate is shown in Figure 2.1 and this, together with the remittance slips from the principal, the front page of the Schedules, all bank statements and any paid bills suffice for the preparation of the annual accounts.

| INCOME MAY 1992 | | | | EXPENDITURE MAY 1992 | | | |
|---|---|---|---|---|---|---|---|
| 12 th | Interest Rcd | 12 | 64 | 1st | Laundry | 6 | 30 |
| 20th | From Principal | 2851 | 31 | 5th | GDC-Subs | 65 | 00 |
| | | | | 9th | Postage | 2 | 40 |
| | | | | 10th | Petrol | 12 | 00 |
| | | | | 15th | Ref. Book | 18 | 50 |
| | | | | 16th | Stationery | 15 | 75 |
| | | | | 17th | Petrol | 10 | 50 |
| | | | | 19th | Telephone | 69 | 70 |
| | | | | 25th | Petrol | 12 | 00 |
| | | | | | | | |
| | | 2863 | 95 | | | 212 | 15 |

Figure 2.1　Associate Cash Book

## The associate and the tax man

Associates do not usually have many problems with the Inland Revenue because their affairs are simple and they handle little, if any, cash. Nevertheless, it has been known for associates to be subjected to an investigation when the principal's affairs have come under scrutiny. It is sensible to maintain proper records and to retain these for at least six years.

Typical expenses that an associate can claim for tax purposes are:

1  Deductions made by the principal for technicians' charges, hygienist fees and bad debts but not for superannuation (this is allowed in a different way).
2  Any dental materials and instruments provided at the associate's own expense.
3  Protective clothing (eg surgery coats and glasses, and laundry) to the extent it is not provided by the principal.
4  Professional subscriptions (GDC, BDA, DPL, MDU, etc.).
5  Professional journals and reference (not text-) books.
6  Courses and conferences to update or maintain knowledge (but not training courses).
7  Any necessary postage, stationery and telephone costs.

8   Modest motor expenses to cover domicillary visits, attendance at courses and professional meetings, visits to the laboratory, bank, etc. Also allowable is the cost of travelling between surgeries, but not the cost of travelling between home and surgery or back (*see* Chapter 17).

9   Accountancy charges (by concession).

10  Any other expenses directly concerned in earning profit.

A specimen income and expenditure account for the year ended 5 April 1991 for an associate follows:

|  | £ | £ |
|---|---|---|
| Fees earned | | 29,493 |
| Dental materials | 42 | |
| Replacement of instruments and | 76 | |
| Maintenance of equipment | | |
| Laundry and protective clothing | 3,397 | |
| Professional subscriptions | 435 | |
| Motor and travelling expenses | 1,694 | |
| Postage and stationery | 12 | |
| Telephone | 206 | |
| Professional journals and reference books | 45 | |
| Bank charges | 60 | |
| Courses and seminars | 20 | |
| Hire purchase charges | 36 | |
| Incidentals | 10 | |
| Superannuation | 1,831 | |
| | £4,929 | |
| EXCESS OF INCOME OVER EXPENDITURE | | £24,564 |

## Ceasing to be an associate

It is probably the ambition of every young associate to become a principal by establishing their own practice or buying an interest in an existing one. Apart from the financial consideration, the wise associate will take into account the tax position arising out of the change of status. Under the complex rules that currently govern assessments, it will often be unwise for an associate to change to principal within five years of starting work as an associate:

Example: Profit for the year to 31 March:

| | |
|---|---|
| 1989 | £19,000 |
| 1990 | £26,000 |
| 1991 | £28,000 |
| 1992 | £29,000 |
| 1993 | £30,000 |
| | £132,000 |

Assessments would be:

| | |
|---|---|
| 1987/88 $(5 \div 365) \times £19,000$ | £260 |
| 1988/89 | £19,000 |
| 1989/90 | £19,000 |
| 1990/91 | £26,000 |
| 1991/92 | £28,000 |
| 1992/93 | £29,000 |
| 1993/94 | £30,000 |

If the practice ceased on 31 March 1993 the assessments would be revised as follows:

|  | Normal basis | Section 63 | Final |
|---|---|---|---|
| 1987/88: as before |  |  | £260 |
| 1988/89: as before |  |  | £19,000 |
| 1989/90: as before |  |  | £19,000 |
| 1990/91: as before | £26,000 |  |  |
| or (5 ÷ 365) × £29,000 |  |  |  |
| + (360 ÷ 365) × £28,000 |  | £28,013* | £28,013 |
| 1991/92: as before | £28,000 |  |  |
| or (5 ÷ 365) × £30,000 |  |  |  |
| + (360 ÷ 365) × £29,000 |  | £29,014* | £29,014 |
| 1992/93: (360 ÷ 365) × £30,000 |  |  | £29,589 |
|  | ———— | ———— | ———— |
|  | £54,000 | £57,027 | £124,876 |

*The Inland Revenue has the option to choose the revised Section 63 TA (1988) if this gives rise to a higher amount taxable (in the opening three years the taxpayer has the option).

In the past it was possible to avoid the cessation provisions which made the exercise counter-productive in tax terms by the argument that the associate is still *de facto* a dental surgeon undertaking the same work, sometimes on the same patients, in the same practice. Whilst this proposition does seem to have some merit, two cases have been before the Special Commissioners of Income Tax (both of which are unfortunately not reported), which rejected the submission. These may not have the same force as a decision in the Court of Appeal but nevertheless they are still taken into account by Inland Revenue staff and by the General Commissioners.

# 3

# Setting up in practice

It is usually the ambition of most practitioners, having completed a period working as an associate, to acquire a practice, or an interest in a practice, and to practise as a principal.

## Starting out

At one time it was quite common for the practitioner to identify an area that lacked adequate dental services and then acquire suitable premises from which to operate. This had the advantage that there was no capital outlay on goodwill. The practitioners could select their own equipment from the outset and would decide their own practice profile. Where it was possible to combine home and surgery together, at least for the time being, this also had the advantage of being easier to control and operate, as well as being less costly. The main disadvantage was that, before advertising rules were relaxed in November 1985, it probably meant a meagre life-style until the patient-base had built up to a reasonable level. To some extent this could be overcome if an associate could continue in the associate position whilst building up their own practice.

The new contract had the potential to virtually bring squatting to an end because patients, having tied themselves for a specified period to a GDP under the capitation or continuing care scheme, were reluctant to change. However, the greater number of practitioners opting out of the NHS scheme has reversed this trend, particularly where the newcomer is willing to undertake NHS treatment. Indeed, FHSAs with an 'area of need' are offering incentives to practitioners willing to establish NHS or mixed practices, and it is often worthwhile discussing the position with the local FHSA before setting up in a particular area.

# Purchasing an existing practice

The most common course, however, is still to purchase an existing practice, either in whole or part. Practices on offer can usually be found:

1 Advertised in the dental press (*The Dentist, Dental Practice, Probe* and *British Dental Journal*).
2 On the books of one of the specialist agencies, of which there are several.
3 In some instances dental supply company representatives become aware of practices for sale before the reach the open market.
4 Very occasionally a direct approach to a practitioner known to be on the point of retirement will bear fruit.

The purchase consideration will take into account four elements

1 The premises (freehold or leasehold).
2 Equipment.
3 Goodwill.
4 Stocks of materials.

## Premises

Property will either be freehold or leasehold. The former is in effect owned by the practitioner, perhaps subject to mortgage. The latter is held under a lease for a predetermined period in return for an annual rent, which can be renewed although care should be taken with some premises (eg a community health centre) where the tenancy is specific to the named practitioner and is not assignable.

### Freehold property

Provided the prospective purchaser arranges for a proper survey and entrusts the conveyancing to a solicitor or licensed conveyancer, there should be little problem in the purchase. The surveyor will be able to identify any structural defects and give some idea as to the property value. These factors can be useful not only for the purpose of raising finance but also in negotiating with the vendor. However, it is wise to ensure the extent of the survey; some purchasers are inclined to accept a cheaper valuation rather than a full structural survey.

Any defects in legal title, adverse planning proposals or failure to obtain proper planning permission, certainly not unknown with dental practices, ought to be revealed in the course of the conveyancing procedure.

*Leasehold property*

Under the terms of a lease the tenant has a right to occupy the premises for a predetermined period in return for an annual rental and possibly, particularly with a premises within a new development, a service charge.

It is prudent to engage the services of a surveyor to advise on the structural aspects of the property. This is particularly important in the case of a full repairing lease, under which the tenant is responsible for structural as well as decorative maintenance. Any tenant would feel very aggrieved if faced with the cost of carrying out repairs to the roof, foundations or drains only a short time after taking over the lease.

It is also important to bear in mind that a lease will usually require the tenant, on expiry or surrender of the lease, to restore the property to its original condition, even though this could well date back a very long way, almost certainly to before the occupation of the final tenant. In consequence, on acquiring a lease it is wise to ask for a copy of the schedule of dilapidations and to take into account anything that will need to be made good.

It might be appropriate to point out at this stage that it is often the case that the obligations of a tenant do not cease on vacating the property; they will continue to be responsible for rent and other outgoings payable by any subsequent tenant in the event of default on their part. This can be overcome by an insurance-backed indemnity cover.

The length of a lease is also an important factor because the value of a lease will amortize (ie depreciate) as time passes and this could well affect the saleability. In effect this amortisation should be regarded as a sort of additional rent to be paid for use of the property. It is, of course, conceivable that the tenant could insist upon renewal of a business premises lease, but there are exceptions to this rule and, in any event, such a right does not determine the future rent payable.

It is prudent to be properly advised by a solicitor or conveyancer experienced in commercial leases throughout the process of buying a leasehold.

Rent is usually reviewed at predetermined intervals and care will need to be taken to ensure that proper notice is served on the landlord at the appropriate time; it may also be necessary to appoint someone suitably qualified to negotiate the new rental.

Service charges are rather more hazardous in that the total running costs of the complex (rates, heating and lighting communal areas, block insurance and maintenance) are divided between tenants. Where managing agents are involved the costs could be difficult to determine in advance, and equally difficult to control. Certainly this factor should be taken into account from the outset.

## Equipment

Inevitably every practitioner has their own preferences for equipment but, having regard to the initial outlay in purchasing a practice, it is perhaps sensible to retain the existing equipment/furnishings until funds become available for replacement. It follows that some consideration should be given to the condition and age of the equipment, and particularly to its life expectancy. Failure to do this could result in the GDP having to unexpectedly replace some items at a time when there is already considerable demand on financial resources. These factors need to be assessed when deciding on an offer price, and it may be desirable to appoint someone such as a dental supplier's representative to propose a value, as such a person is most likely to be acquainted with current prices for new and used equipment. The same individual may also be later used in the stock-taking process.

All too often a purchaser is so anxious to get started that they will accept the figure proposed by the vendor, or, worse still, simply accept the proposed figure from one valuer, without seeking other valuations.

Two further points that are frequently overlooked by an intending purchaser are:

1   The need to obtain a detailed inventory of equipment, showing serial numbers or other identification, before contracts are exchanged. It is not unknown for an unscrupulous vendor to exchange the equipment once a sale has been agreed. He may be a 'nice chap' but it is best to leave nothing to chance.
2   An assurance that the equipment price includes all the hand instruments and handpieces, unless these are to be taken into consideration in the stock valuation.

It is, of course, sensible to ask a solicitor to check what equipment is on lease, lease purchase, hire purchase or otherwise not the property of the vendor. The intention as to clearing any debt is also pertinent, because no purchaser will wish to be faced with a claim from a finance company for equipment believed to have been purchased outright.

## Goodwill

This is defined as:

> The privilege granted by the seller of a business to the purchaser of trading as a recognized successor; the possession of a ready formed connection of customers considered as a separate element in the saleable value of a business.

Goodwill is probably the most difficult part of the dental practice to value. Traditionally, it has been the practice to assess the goodwill value at between 30 and 40% of the gross average fee income over the preceding three years; the lower figure being for a wholly NHS practice and the latter figure for a wholly private practice. A mixed practice will lie somewhere between the two parameters.

As goodwill is really little more than the sum a willing purchaser is prepared to pay to a willing vendor for the benefit of potential earning capacity of the practice, it is something that will command a lower sum where there is a surfeit of practices on the market. A wide range of other issues will also affect the value of goodwill:

1   The size of the capitation and continuing care list.
2   The ratio between completed and uncompleted restorative work for children under capitation, for whom entry payments have been claimed and cannot be claimed again under the 'same dentist' rule.
3   Specialist practice, eg orthodontics, periodontics, etc.
4   Local competition. A surgery located in a prime high street position is likely to present a better purchase than one in a more isolated area; one located alongside a host of other practices is likely to be less attractive than one located on its own.
5   The basis on which the average fee income has been calculated. If the period taken into account included something unusual, such as a high child entry income, this needs to be adjusted.
6   The appearance of the surgery. At the present time patients tend to vote with their feet and are less likely to come to a down-at-heel practice, particularly when the known practitioner has moved on.
7   The reasons for sale could well be pertinent. It may be that the vendors can forsee a downturn in patients, or perhaps they are opening elsewhere in the area. In either of these cases the goodwill would be at risk.

It should always be borne in mind that there can be a loss of up to 20% of the patients through no reason other than a change in ownership; but equally, the incoming practitioner will start to create goodwill with new patients. Always insist that the vendor should enter into a 'barring out' agreement.

*Practices limited to a speciality*

These practices have their own peculiarities which affect the goodwill:

1   They are not always so readily saleable, because there are fewer potential buyers.
2   In some types of referral practice there is less 'repeat' attendance compared to a general practice. Different specialities attract different levels of repeat attendance. For example, there is more scope for multiple attendance in a periodontology referral practice than, say, an endodontic practice.
3   In some cases the retiring practitioner will need to sign off NHS work, which attracted direct payment, and the incoming practitioner will be left with the less profitable end of the work.
4   Goodwill may be more associated with the individual practitioner rather than the 'practice' site.

A more realistic method of assessing goodwill in an orthodontic practice, for example, would be to consider the profit element rather than the new income. Adjusting the known average profits to allow for the sort of salary the incoming practitioner might expect to command will produce a super profit, which is that part of the profit that represents a return on the overall investment in property, equipment and goodwill.

Thus, for example, a practice showing £75,000 net profit for a practitioner who might reasonably expect a salary of £45,000 per annum, would be showing a super profit of £30,000. At a sensible rate of return, bearing in mind the commercial risks involved, at 6% this would require an investment of half a million pounds.

After deducting the value of the property and equipment, the balance remaining would represent goodwill, although this ought to be reduced by between 12 and 15% to allow for the personal contact that the vendor would have had with local GDPs.

The problems with valuing goodwill for an in-house laboratory will be dealt with in Chapter 24.

## Stock of materials

The valuation of materials (and, if appropriate, of instruments) is also best left to a representative from a dental supply company. The main point to watch out for is the inclusion of obsolete stock or items which have an expired shelf life. Many practitioners see the disposal of their practice as the ideal time to off-load stock that is no longer usable; equally, the over-anxious purchaser will tend to accept this situation and complain later. It is best resolved at the time.

# Staff

Where a GDP acquires an existing practice it is often forgotten that the staff represent a part of the deal. A change in employer does not affect the length of service for the purpose of holidays or for sick, maternity and redundancy pay. It follows that should it become necessary to dismiss a member of staff, and it must always be borne in mind that the receptionists or DSAs may resent a newcomer with new methods, a claim to redundancy pay could arise.

In the past there have been abortive attempts to avoid this obligation by dismissing and re-engaging staff. To be effective any break must be measured in months rather than weeks.

By far the best method is for the incoming GDP to be given adequate compensation in the purchase price to allow for both accrued holidays yet to be taken and also for potential redundancy pay claims, after all, the vendor would have to make such payments if they were required to dismiss the staff.

Care ought to be taken to ensure that all clinical records are handed over on completion (even if a right of access is still to be permitted) and it might also be prudent to arrange with the retiring practitioner for a joint letter to be circulated to all patients, irrespective of anything that might be issued by the FHSA. This is likely to create a better impression with the patients.

Where the practice is contracted to a dental health scheme it may be appropriate to consider the implications for individual patients, and also to review the fee scale. The purchaser should also check to see if there are any problems over treatment. For example, has the vendor taken the fee but neglected the patient's needs, leaving the purchaser to deal with them?

In the case of any equipment continuing on lease, it is prudent to ensure that the leasing companies are notified and agree to the change.

Gas, electricity and water meters should be read at the point of change and the vendor should leave a forwarding address.

Whilst the matter of taxation is dealt with in greater depth in Chapter 15, it might be appropriate to comment here that for tax purposes the vendor will seek a lower figure on equipment and a higher portion of the purchase price for property and goodwill; to the purchaser the reverse is desirable, and it is important that these figures are not only agreed at the time but also clearly set out in the assignment documents. This will save arguments at a later date.

# Legal costs

Purchasers often under-estimate the cost of acquiring a new practice. Apart from the legal costs and expenses, there will be costs relating to the move itself, including any additional equipment or redecorations. It is sensible to obtain a clear estimate for all this expenditure from the outset.

# 4

# Employing staff

The payroll is undoubtedly the largest expense in any dental practice, and the staff are the most important asset. The receptionist will be the first point of contact for the patient making an appointment, be it in person or on the telephone. The reputation of a practice may be enhanced or destroyed through the impression created by reception staff.

The DSA is equally important, and is looked upon as a support by nervous patients; their reaction can calm or agitate the patient. The DSA can also help or hinder the practitioner.

Sadly, few GDPs pay sufficient attention to this area of their practice, and are more influenced by staffing costs than by the quality of staff. All too often too much is left to chance, both in the area of recruitment and training as well as in the area of adequate paperwork. In most instances this is because the GDPs are trained as clinicians rather than managers, even though they run business operations.

Often, much of the paperwork and administration is left to the GDP's spouse, who again may have no formal training. Over-protection by the spouse may create staff unrest and a high rate of staff turnover. In cases where dentist-staff relationships are compromised by the spouse, it may be prudent for the spouse to assume a less active interest in the practice.

It is also sometimes argued that the GDP's relationship with staff is a personal matter, into which the law should not intrude. This is not the case but, as a result of this attitude, many practitioners find themselves in a situation of conflict that could well result in the involvement of an Industrial Tribunal and the risk of substantial penalties.

## Staff recruitment

Selection of the right staff for the job will not only lead to a smoothly and efficiently run practice but it will also minimize staff turnover due to dismissal or resignation. Before setting out to appoint staff the GDP should ask what sort of individual is needed.

Inevitably the starting point is the job description, from which it should be possible to evaluate the skills and personal attributes desirable in a candidate.

*Suggested skills for a receptionist*

1 Pleasant and cheerful personality.
2 Ability to remain placid in a crisis or in a situation of confrontation with a patient.
3 Training in telephone techniques.
4 Neat handwriting.
5 Careful attention to detail.
6 Ability to be both accurate and methodical.
7 Confidentiality.

*Suggested skills for a practice manager*

1 The same skills as for a receptionist.
2 The ability to handle and control staff.
3 Readiness to undertake any administrative task, but also the ability to delegate responsibility to someone else.
4 Tact in dealing with staff personal problems and the ability to handle a disciplinary situation.
5 Absolute loyalty to the principal and to the practice.
6 Confidentiality.
7 An understanding of the legal requirements (the NHS regulations, employment legislation etc.).
8 An understanding of accounts, particularly the control of finance and maintenance of proper accounting records.
9 Understanding of PAYE, banking and insurance procedures.
10 An appreciation of the operation and rules of dental health schemes (where appropriate).
11 Dedication to the practice philosophy.

*Suggested skills for a surgery DSA*

1 Cheerful disposition and neat presentation.
2 High standards of hygiene.
3 The ability to remain calm in a crisis and to instil confidence in the patient.
4 An understanding of dental techniques, materials, instruments and equipment.
5 Care in handling costly materials and avoiding waste.
6 The ability to act as part of a clinical team, being in the right place with the correct instruments and materials at the proper time, effectively a sound understanding of the GDP's work and preferences.
7 Confidentiality.

It is true that some of these skills will be acquired with training but there must be core qualities which allow the candidate to acquire or add to them.

Unfortunately, many practitioners are inclined to add a further quality to the list in each case – the candidate must be cheap – and this can well prove counter productive in the long term, as it could lead to staff discontent, high staff turnover and repetition of training costs.

## Where to recruit

Having decided the type of person needed, the GDP must then consider where to recruit applicants. This may be:

1   By advertisement in the local press or, especially where technically qualified staff are needed, through the dental press.
2   Through the local Jobcentre, although here it is essential to ensure that there is a clear understanding about the qualities and experience sought otherwise much time can be wasted interviewing unsuitable candidates.
3   Through an employment agency, which will usually vet prospective candidates and prepare a short-list of suitable applicants. It is necessary to bear in mind that a fee will be payable for this service but in practice it could be money well spent.
4   Very occasionally a practitioner might engage in 'head hunting' by approaching a suitable employee working for a colleague by offering a higher salary.
5   In the case of very junior staff it is sometimes possible that a school leaver can be recruited either by a direct approach to the local school or by engaging someone who has been on a work experience assignment in the practice.

It may be useful to use a standard type of application form to ensure uniformity.

In consultation with the practice manager, a short-list of suitable applicants should be prepared for interview. The interview itself should be a formal affair, held on the premises, and notes should be retained for subsequent discussion. It is unwise to notify the outcome until all candidates have been interviewed and then a letter sent to each advising of the decision.

The successful candidate should be sent a letter of offer setting out the terms and conditions, job description, rate of pay and date of commencement of the employment.

# Staff training

Probably the most neglected area of training is that of induction for a new employee, who is all too often introduced to fellow workers and then left to learn about the practice as best they can. In an efficient practice, however, the practice manager will devote time to explaining the procedures and peculiarities of the practice, the location of supplies and the duties of other members of the team. It is an opportunity to ensure that the new employee is acquainted with the tasks and given the information necessary to enable them to fit into the team quickly and efficiently.

The question of skill training, for example the use of the computers, word processors or fax, will depend on individual circumstances.

Quite clearly it is sensible to ensure that staff are properly trained in any new skills required of them because this will lead to a greater efficiency in the shortest possible time; in most cases money spent on training is well spent.

# Contracts of employment

As soon as an employee is engaged there is a contract of employment in existence, although the law does not require it to be in a written format until three months after commencement. This does not normally apply to part-time staff working for less than 16 hours each week, except where the individual has consistently worked for an average of more than eight hours each week for at least five years.

A number of proprietary forms can be used for a written contract but any GDP is at liberty to produce their own staff contract. The essential elements are:

1    The name and address of the employer.
2    The name and address of the employee.
3    Job description, eg receptionist, DSA, etc.
4    Brief summary of duties.
5    Rate of pay.
6    Hours of work.
7    Holiday arrangements and pay.
8    Any provisions concerning sick pay.
9    Period of termination notice required.
10   Grievance, disciplinary and appeals procedure.

Some practitioners go further than is strictly demanded by law, even to the extent of producing a staff handbook setting out arrangements for reviewing pay, identification of individual 'perks' and explaining the internal systems and procedures.

Whilst a written contract will not avoid disputes it will certainly minimize the risk of a dispute ending up before an Industrial Tribunal, and will go a long way to providing the basis for a settlement. In the event of a dispute coming before an Industrial Tribunal, a written contract and evidence of effort to comply with the law would certainly be to the credit of the GDP.

The employee does not necessarily have to sign the contract for it to be valid. However, any changes in the terms and conditions of employment will need to be negotiated separately, although, where these do not erode the conditions of service, it is unlikely that any difficulties will arise.

It is sensible that the job description should be fairly flexible to cope with changing situations, and it would certainly be wise to ensure that the job title was not unduly rigid.

There are no statutory provisions regarding rates of pay, which will vary from one area to another, and it is perhaps wise to see what rates are offered by colleagues in a similar situation.

Likewise, there are no standard requirements as regards holiday pay and, again, it is sensible to see what is done in other local practices before making a decision. Usually a member of staff will expect the statutory public holidays together with two or three weeks paid leave to be taken by arrangement.

## Staff records

In the majority of practices there is no proper system for staff records, and this will create problems, especially when letters or other documents are lost and there is no independent record of information (eg salary changes, training or holiday records, etc.). The sensible course would be to maintain a file for each member of staff containing:

1   The original employment application, interview notes, a copy of the advertisement, references taken up and letter of appointment.
2   A record of any changes in job description and duties with appropriate dates.
3   A history of salary changes with dates.
4   A record of sickness and dates.
5   Any correspondence concerning the employee.
6   Details, with dates, of training courses and examination results.
7   Where oral or written warnings have been given the file should contain full details and original documents.

8    A copy of the letter of dismissal or resignation and, in the latter case, a note of the reasons.

Such a file will prove invaluable in the event of any problems and should be retained indefinitely where it cannot be accessed by any other employee except the practice manager. In most cases proprietary forms are available that meet these requirements.

## Dismissal

Dismissal often occurs when an employee has had to be given warning about some form of misconduct. Except in the case of theft or other criminal offence, the employee is entitled to be given oral and then written warning before dismissal. All too often cases end up before an Industrial Tribunal because the GDP has neglected to follow the proper procedures. It is wise for a note of an oral warning, indicating the circumstances, date and any witnesses, to be kept on the staff file, and that a copy of any subsequent written warning is likewise retained.

Generally speaking, an employee cannot complain of unfair dismissal if they have been employed for less than two years after the age of 18 years at the time of dismissal, and have been engaged for fewer than 16 hours each week (subject to the exception mentioned earlier).

This will also apply in the case of an employee over the statutory retirement age, which is 65 years for men and 60 years for women.

Redundancy pay can be claimed where an employee's job has come to an end, but care must be taken to ensure that no one else is appointed to undertake the same work, because that would prejudice the claim that the job was redundant and could lead to a claim for unfair or wrongful dismissal. The constraints that apply to an unfair dismissal claim usually also apply to redundancy claims.

Where there is a voluntary resignation the reasons should be noted: where there is a high staff turnover the cause needs to be identified and rectified.

## Statutory maternity rights

This is something that affects dental practices that employ young women; it may well cause difficulties. Generally speaking the expectant mother has four statutory rights:

1   Not to be refused reasonable paid leave for antenatal care.
2   To receive her Statutory Maternity Pay (SMP), if she has worked for the same employer for more than 26 weeks at more than the lower National Insurance (NI) limit.
3   Not to be dismissed as a result of the pregnancy; this could constitute a claim for unfair dismissal.
4   To return to work with the employer after absence due to pregnancy and confinement.

Because the provisions are complex it is important that the individual responsible for the payroll within the practice should be conversant with SMP regulations. A breach of the regulations could land the GDP unwittingly before an Industrial Tribunal, with costly consequences. The Department of Social Security (DSS) has published a booklet, *An Employer's Guide to Statutory Maternity Pay,* and the wise practitioner will ensure that a copy is held in the surgery office.

## Statutory sick pay

The DSS no longer handles sick pay claims, except in certain circumstances. This work is now put on to the shoulders of the GDP and, as with most government regulations, the situation is complicated. All practices should ensure that they hold a copy of the DSS publication *An Employer's Guide to Statutory Sick Pay.* Broadly, the rules are:

1   An employer has to pay Statutory Sick Pay (SSP) and reclaim it later by deduction when remitting Pay As You Earn (PAYE) or NI contributions.
2   SSP is liable for the same deductions in respect of tax and NI as the normal salary.
3   The employer decides what SSP should be paid (there are three rates) and is responsible for any errors.
4   After 28 weeks the employer ceases to make the payment and the task is then assumed by the DSS.

Normally the employee is not entitled to be paid for the first four days of sick leave in a period of 8 weeks, although the employer may pay the employee if they so wish. During this four-day period the employee is entitled to self-certify sickness, the DSS provides suitable forms for this.

# Statutory deductions

There is a temptation for some employers to pay 'cash in hand' without deductions for tax or national insurance. This is often done from petty cash in the case of cleaners or gardeners, the argument being that they would otherwise not be willing to work. However, it is also sometimes done in the case of a DSA's overtime or additional duties of a receptionist/clerk.

*Such practices are unlawful and are not to be recommended.* The only cases in which it is lawful not to deduct tax or NI are those where the employee has signed Certificate B on form P46, stating that they have no other employment. Although, statutorily, it is necessary to get such a form signed only once, it is sensible to obtain a fresh form for each tax year because circumstances do change and a new certificate will act as an insurance to the GDP if challenged.

Where, on a PAYE Audit visit by either the Inland Revenue or DSS, cases are identified where tax and NI should have been deducted but this has not been done, the employer may be liable to make good both the tax and NI lost (and could even be faced with interest and penalties), with no redress against the employee due to the operation of the Truck Acts, which preclude any right to make a retrospective deduction from pay.

The wise course is, irrespective of the difficulties, to operate the PAYE/NI system properly.

# Benefits in kind

Some practitioners seek to avoid tax or NI for employees by a variety of practices, many of which are of dubious character. The same caution applies here as for untaxed pay because penalties and interest will almost certainly be imposed when the practice comes to light.

It is permissible to give an employee a tax-free gift provided it cannot be converted into a cash equivalent (a gift voucher would not fall within this category because it is effectively cash) but even so it is sensible to keep the gift to reasonable value – about £25 to £30 would be a sensible limit.

The idea of paying hairdressing bills or similar is to be avoided; and the provision of a domestic telephone service or the use of a 'company car' for a receptionist is likely to attract unwelcome attention with the attendant risks.

It is, however, permissible for the practice to pay for laundry of overalls, and even to supply protective clothing, provided it is regarded as essential to the job.

# Spouse's salary

For a spouse's salary to be regarded as a legitimate expense against the practice profits, it must:

1   Be reasonable, ie it must represent a fair commercial rate for the job undertaken.
2   Actually have been paid, either at the time or at the worst no more than nine months after the end of the financial year.

This issue frequently gives rise to problems in practice and is becoming of greater interest to the Inland Revenue, along with untaxed pay and benefits in kind.

# Staff parties

As a concession, the Inland Revenue will allow the GDP to deduct for tax purposes the cost of one annual dinner or similar function, provided the cost does not exceed £50 per head, for employees. Staff lunches and other social activities are not deductible, although it is unlikely that, other than in exceptional circumstances, the Inland Revenue would seek to charge the employee as a benefit in kind.

# Health and safety at work

The GDP is required under the Health and Safety at Work Etc Act (1974) to provide and maintain a safe working environment. Except where there are fewer than five employees, the employer has to provide a written statement of general policy on health and safety, and is also required to ensure there is adequate information, training and supervision of staff.

The main issues affecting the GDP are

1   Fire regulations.
2   First-aid and resuscitation procedures.
3   Control of substances hazardous to health (COSHH).
4   The reporting of injuries, diseases and dangerous occurences (RIDDOR) regulations (1989).
5   Electricity at work regulations (1989).
6   Water regulations.
7   Pressure systems/transportable gas container regulations.

8   Laser regulations.
9   Cross-infection control measures.
10  Ionizing radiation regulations (1988).

The GDP should address each of these issues to ensure that the practice conforms to current standards. Advice and up-to-date guidance is available from the British Dental Association.

# The hygienist, dental therapist and educator

There is a growing tendency for routine dental hygiene and education to be entrusted to a hygienist. The work will either be carried out on the dentist's own FHSA number or on a fee-paying basis by the patient. The hygienist is usually paid:

1   On a sessional basis, irrespective of the number of patients treated.
2   At an hourly rate, also irrespective of the number of treatments.
3   On a percentage basis of the fees earned.
4   On a per capita basis.

Hygienists are usually treated as self-employed subcontractors, because this enables them to claim tax relief for expenses against their earnings. This tax relief might not be available to an employee.

The GDP will probably readily accede to such a request as it will save employer's NI contribution and will avoid the hazards of employment legislation. In reality, this is almost certainly an ill-conceived assumption, which could easily create more problems than it solves; certainly it is unlikely to hold out on an Inland Revenue or DSS inspection visit. Broadly speaking, the tests applied to identify the self-employed are:

1   Does the individual contract directly with the patients?
2   Is the treatment carried out on the surgery premises?
3   Who provides the instruments, equipment and materials?
4   Is there any measure of supervision of the work by a qualified dental practitioner?
5   How is the pay calculated, is it related directly to the volume and complexity of the work carried out?
6   Who bears the bad debts?
7   Is the hygienist taking any commercial risks (apart from that of a possible negligence claim)?
8   What would be the response if the hygienist either did not wish to treat a particular patient or decided for some reason not to do the work herself but to delegate it to another suitable qualified deputy?

Consideration of these points would probably point firmly to the fact that the hygienist is under the control and direction of the GDP, as is any other employee. It is not sufficient to claim that a hygienist works for more than one practitioner, because it is open to any employee to have more than one employer simultaneously.

In the majority of cases, therefore, the GDP should deduct tax and NI from the hygienist's pay and the hygienist should negotiate direct with the Inland Revenue over expenses. Failure to do so could well result in a claim for back tax and NI, as well as for interest and penalties.

## The associate

It could be argued that the associate is in a similar position to the hygienist, but this is not really so. Associates have the clinical freedom to carry out what treatment they think necessary and in the way they think best. They will also have their own FHSA number and consequently have a direct contract with the patient and the FHSA. The position of the associate has not yet been challenged by the Inland Revenue, although it remains a possibility.

# 5

# Stock control

One of the most neglected areas in any dental surgery is proper stock control. As a result, few practitioners can know exactly what materials or instruments they have on hand, or the rate at which these items are being consumed.

All too often a surgery is over-stocked with materials for which the shelf life has long expired. This is because a practitioner, keen to save money, is attracted by special offers and will purchase quantities that are in excess of needs.

It is important to bear in mind that an overstocked surgery can create difficulties:

1   Far too much money may be tied up in stock when in reality suppliers are but a telephone call away and supplies can be replenished at short notice.
2   The problem of excess stock is is exacerbated where practitioners in the same premises use too wide a range of materials when some standardisation would facilitate more economic purchasing methods.
3   Inadequate housekeeping or stock rotation can easily result in stock being allowed to pass its 'sell-by' date, with the result that it has to be discarded as obsolete.
4   Some items are prone to theft by their very nature, and a laissez-faire attitude to stock control means that the way is open to any dishonest individual seeking to build up stocks for their own new surgery.
5   Valuable space is taken up for storage.
6   Staff are inclined to be extravagant where stock appears plentiful.

The majority of practitioners feel that they can control stock without any paperwork, but it is likely that time spent by a practice manager in this area of the practice will reap rewards by:

1   Ensuring that only minimum stock levels are held, thereby releasing capital for other purposes.
2   Keeping a check on the rate of consumption in each individual surgery, which will assist costing.

3    Identify consumption levels and so eliminate waste.
4    Provide reasonably accurate figures of stock levels in the annual
     accounts, thereby making these more accurate and valuable for
     management purposes.

All supplies should be kept in a separate locked cupboard under the
control of the practice manager or a responsible DSA. No-one else should
be allowed access and no-one else should order goods.

A stock card should be held for each individual stock line and kept up
to date by the key holder. By this means there is a record of the stock
received, issued and held together with the values (Figure 5.1).

| Stock Card  21 | | | | Maximum Stock Level  1000 | | | | | |
| --- | --- | --- | --- | --- | --- | --- | --- | --- | --- |
| Description  *LATEX EXAMINATION* | | | | Minimum Stock Level    300 | | | | | |
| *GLOVES* | | | | Re-Order Level           400 | | | | | |
| | | | | Re-Order Quantity    600 | | | | | |
| DATE | ISSUE | RECEIVED | BALANCE | ISSUE | | RECEIVED | | BALANCE | |
| 1·4·92 | | b/fwd | 500 | £ | p | £ | p | £ | p |
| 10·4·92 | 50 | | 450 | 2 | 00 | | | 18 | 00 |
| 17·4·92 | 50 | | 400 | 2 | 00 | | | 16 | 00 |
| 19·4·92 | 100 | | 300 | 4 | 00 | | | 12 | 00 |
| 25·4·92 | | 600 | 900 | | | 24 | 00 | 36 | 00 |
| | | | | | | | | | |
| | | | | | | | | | |
| | | | | | | | | | |
| | | | | | | | | | |
| | | | | | | | | | |
| SUPPLIER  A BC  Supplies Ltd. | | | | | | | | | |

Figure 5.1   Stock Card

Whilst stock may be charged out to the surgery on a number bases, the best pricing method is probably 'averaging', in which the value of a new delivery is added to the value of existing stocks and the resultant figure is divided by the total stock held to arrive at a 'charge out' rate.

The deliveries of new supplies should be added to the stock card and the charge out price should be adjusted accordingly. For example:

|  |  | Total |
|---|---|---|
| Existing stock | 20 units at £1.00 | £20.00 |
| New delivery | 10 units at £1.50 | £15.00 |
|  | 30 units | £35.00 |

The issue price has increased from £1 per unit to £35/30 = £1.17

Once an individual surgery has been fully stocked with materials and hand instruments, nothing further should be issued without a requisition being presented. By this means it will be possible to clearly identify the consumption by each practitioner and, if the requisitions are priced and retained, it will be possible to place a value on such consumption.

| MATERIALS REQUISITION NOTE | | | |
|---|---|---|---|
| DATE REQUIRED 19·4·92 | SURGERY No 2 | | |
| DESCRIPTION | ISSUED | £ | P |
| Latex Examination Gloves | 100 | 4 | 00 |
|  |  |  |  |
|  |  |  |  |
|  |  |  |  |
|  |  |  |  |
|  |  |  |  |
| Signed J. Pullen. | Date 19·4·92 | | |

Figure 5.2   Materials Requisition Note

# 6

# Equipment: lease or purchase?

Practitioners frequently ask their accountants whether it is better to lease or purchase equipment; but the answer is not always a simple one. Basically there are several ways in which capital equipment can be acquired:

1   Outright purchase, either with cash or a bank loan.
2   On hire purchase.
3   Under a lease-purchase agreement.
4   By leasing it.

## Outright purchase

In this case the practitioner becomes the immediate owner of the equipment concerned and is, therefore, free to do what they will with it. However, it does mean tying up capital, be it the free funds of the practice or borrowed from the bank, to effect the purchase.

This does, of course, have a cost, either in terms of opportunity cost, which is the loss of the use of the capital for other purposes (eg as an interest generating investment) or in terms of interest on the bank loan. The extent of this cost will depend upon what would otherwise be done with the money or the rate of interest charged by the bank. In the majority of cases, however, outright purchase is by far the cheapest method of acquiring equipment.

## Hire purchase

Under the terms of a hire purchase agreement the practitioner will hire the equipment from a finance company for a period of up to three years and will then usually purchase it outright by payment of the option to purchase sum specified in the agreement.

As the finance company itself is usually borrowing the money from bankers, the hire purchase charges are likely to be higher than a bank loan; often the true rate is 18.5% per annum.

It is perhaps wise to remember that the charges levied by the finance company are not interest, and consequently there is no right to a pro rata reduction for early settlement, although some allowances may be given.

## Lease purchase

This is almost identical to a hire purchase agreement but there are no constraints about repossession in the event of non-payment of the leasing instalments. There is also the point that the lease rent will include VAT at the prevailing rate, whereas with a hire purchase agreement the VAT is included in the original cost of plant, as it is with a cash purchase. The agreement will contain an option that may or may not be exercised at the discretion of the hirer. Where it is not exercised a secondary rental (usually a notional amount) will be charged.

## Lease agreement

This, as the name suggests, is a straightforward leasing of the equipment over a given period, after which the rent is reduced to a minimal level. There is no purchase option and theoretically the hirer can never acquire ownership although, in practice, they can usually purchase the equipment through a third party once the primary rental has been cleared.

## Taxation

There are, of course, tax implications, both as regards income tax and VAT. Figure 6.1will clarify the position and indicate comparable figures.

| | Outlay | Hire Purchase | | | Lease Purchase | |
|---|---|---|---|---|---|---|
| | | Tax relief on | | | | |
| | | Capital | Charges | | Outlay | Tax Relief on |
| 1 | £455.20 | | | | £493.74 | £493.74 |
| 2 | £455.20 | | | | £493.74 | £493.74 |
| 3 | £455.20 | | | | £493.74 | £493.74 |
| 4 | £455.20 | | | | £493.74 | £493.74 |
| 5 | £455.20 | | | | £493.74 | £493.74 |
| 6 | £455.20 | | | | £493.74 | £493.74 |
| 7 | £455.20 | | | | £493.74 | £493.74 |
| 8 | £455.20 | | | | £493.74 | £493.74 |
| 9 | £455.20 | | | | £493.74 | £493.74 |
| 10 | £455.20 | | | | £493.74 | £493.74 |
| 11 | £455.20 | | | | £493.74 | £493.74 |
| 12 | £455.20 | £2,500.00 | £462.40 | | £493.74 | £493.74 |
| 13 | £455.20 | | | | £493.74 | £493.74 |
| 14 | £455.20 | | | | £493.74 | £493.74 |
| 15 | £455.20 | | | | £493.74 | £493.74 |
| 16 | £455.20 | | | | £493.74 | £493.74 |
| 17 | £455.20 | | | | £493.74 | £493.74 |
| 18 | £455.20 | | | | £493.74 | £493.74 |
| 19 | £455.20 | | | | £493.74 | £493.74 |
| 20 | £455.20 | | | | £493.74 | £493.74 |
| 21 | £455.20 | | | | £493.74 | £493.74 |
| 22 | £455.20 | | | | £493.74 | £493.74 |
| 23 | £455.20 | | | | £493.74 | £493.74 |
| 24 | £455.20 | £1,875.00 | £462.40 | | £493.74 | £493.74 |
| | | | | | | |
| | £10,924.80 | *£4,375.00 | £924.80 | | £11,849.76 | £11,849.76 |

*Continuing for up to 31 years

**Figure 6.1**   Equipment £10,000 over 2 years

# 7

# Banking

The GDP will almost certainly need the services of a bank for the operation of a practice. In the majority of cases the facility of the lending banker will be of paramount importance but others, more particularly the long-established practitioner, will simply need the straightforward banking facilities.

As the GDP's career develops so too will their demands on the banking fraternity. Usually GDPs make their first contact with a bank during their student days, when they have perhaps looked to the bank to supplement their educational grant. On qualifying, the GDP will seek help in purchasing a motor car and later a home. Then, on becoming a principal, the requirements will expand from the simple loan to the wider range of banking services.

As the relationship between banker and customer is akin to that which the GDP enjoys with his other professional advisers, frequent changes are not to be welcomed. Even so, in recent years with the banks becoming more commercially minded, many GDPs have felt it sensible to 'shop around' for more competitive rates and for a similar range of services at a lower cost.

The building society cheque account had tended to come to the forefront, as has the National Girobank; both inventions of the past twenty years or so. The range of services offered by these institutions is now very much like that offered by the traditional high-street banks.

## Current account

This is the account on which the customer can operate a cheque book. It is of immense value to every GDP as a means of receiving monies (the FHSA payments and those of most of the dental health schemes are paid through the giro system direct into the bank) and for paying bills.

The costs of operating an account will vary between banks, and it is always best to ascertain the charges in advance. In the case of an overdraft, the banks demand an arrangement fee depending on the amount of the facility; an unauthorized overdraft can be very expensive and may result in cheques being dishonoured.

By prior arrangement, the GDP can have overdraft facilities on a current account and so will be able to overdraw the balance when the need arises:

Example: specimen bank charges:

|  | Authorized borrowing | Unauthorized borrowing |
|---|---|---|
| Withdrawals | 75p per item | |
| Credits | 75p per item | |
| Standing charge | £2.50 per month | |
| Returned cheques | £4 | £25 |
| Stopped cheque | £8 | |
| Copy bank statement | £6 | |
| Direct debit | £5 | |
| Status enquiry | £7 plus VAT | |
| Management charge | £55 per hour | |
| Arrangement fee | 1% of the advance | |
| Facility excess | | £5 |
| Letter/telephone advice | £10 | |

The security demanded for an overdraft will also vary considerably. Some banks are sufficiently keen to attract the professional customer that they will allow limited unsecured facilities; others will wish to see the whole debt covered and may also demand insurance on the life of the customer as an added security.

Generally speaking, banks are now apprehensive about lending to dental surgeons and are looking rather more closely at capital gearing in the practices, a subject dealt with in greater detail in Chapter 13.

A private bank account can usually be operated without charges provided it is kept in credit, and interest may be allowed on the balance in the account. Where this is the case, the GDP would be well advised to have two separate accounts so that they do not pay the business account scale of charges on private expenditure or deposits if this can be avoided.

Bank statements are issued at fairly regular intervals and should be carefully preserved, as should the properly completed cheque- and paying-in-book counterfoils. All too often a practitioner throws away bank statements and subsequent finds it necessary to purchase duplicates from the bank at considerable expense.

Likewise, the absence of cheque counterfoils or the omission of information from them may necessitate asking the bank to search out the original cheques, which is an expensive operation as charges will be levied on a time basis. To trace the source of monies paid into the account after the event is virtually impossible.

## Loan accounts

Sometimes a bank will insist that where a GDP wishes to borrow money, for example for purchase of a car, for equipment or even for the purchase of a share in a practice, the funds are advanced on a separate loan account repayable over a fixed period of time. This can either be by a fixed monthly sum credited against the amount of the loan with interest being charged to the account quarterly, or it may be dealt with by dividing the monthly instalment between capital and interest. In this latter case it is easier to see the progress of the loan reductions, which will be smaller at the outset but which will escalate as the capital is repaid and the interest reduced accordingly.

Sometimes the rate of interest on a loan may be higher and on other occasions lower than that charged on a bank overdraft. It is, therefore, difficult to determine which is the cheaper method of borrowing, although terms can be discussed at the time the loan is negotiated.

Again, some loans will be unsecured, although this is rare. More often the bank will require security in the form of a charge over property, life assurance or a personal guarantee. Much will depend upon the GDP's record with the bank and how the bankers view their account.

It is important to note that, where a bank lends money against security of the dentist's residence which is in the joint names of the dentist and their spouse, the spouse should be advised to obtain independent legal advice on the matter, and the documentation will usually be sent to a solicitor for this purpose.

## Deposit account

It may be wise for a practitioner to move surplus funds from their current account and into a deposit account. Sometimes the bank will operate a system whereby the current account is kept at a fixed daily balance and any surplus funds are transferred to overnight deposits. Where the funds retained are substantial (not a common occurrence with dentists) the bank may place them on Treasury Deposits for a period of a month or more at fairly high interest rates. Where this is done, the GDP should be careful to retain the original paperwork for reference purposes, any failure to do this may cause difficulty in reconciling the figures at a later date.

## Giro transfers

In many instances it is more economical for the dentist not to issue an individual cheque to each supplier or employee but to arrange for an internal transfer of funds within the banking system. For this purpose the GDP will need to know:

1   The full name of the supplier (or employee).
2   The name and address of the supplier's (or employee's) bankers.
3   The bank sorting code.
4   The account number.

It is then simply a matter of completing a form supplied by the bank and handing it over with a single cheque payable to the bank, which will then arrange a transfer of the appropriate funds into the correct accounts.

Where this is done it is most important that the practitioner should retain a clear copy of the schedule that has been handed to the bank, or it will later be difficult to ascertain how the single cheque was made up and this can make it impossible to evidence payment of individual bills.

## Joint account

In the case of a dental 'partnership' it will be necessary to have a joint account to collect individual contributions and to pay the pooled expenses. This account should be set up so as to require the signature of all parties, as this will act as a security against misappropriation of funds by a colleague. However, this precaution is voided if signed blank cheques are left in a cheque book.

## Share dealing

Most banks have facilities for the purchase and sale of shares for a customer, but it may be sensible for a GDP with adequate funds for investment to use an independent stockbroker who will also give independent advice on investments.

# Investment advice and life insurance or pensions

Again, the GDP should consider using an independent broker, as their bank will usually be tied to its own products, which may not be the best on the market. An independent broker is required to give best advice and, since the Financial Services Act (1986) all brokers are controlled by a separate regulatory body, such as FIMBRA.

# Trusts and wills

Most banks operate a Trustee Department, which will handle wills and trusts (as well as advising on personal tax matters). There is no doubt that, in the former area, a bank will offer an excellent service, although it can be expensive. However, as banks are large commercial organisations, they frequently lack the personal knowledge and service of the GDP's own solicitor or accountant.

No practitioner should fail to make a will, which should be revised at regular intervals, depending on changing circumstances. Apart from anything else, it does ensure that a widow(er) is not left with unnecessary problems and that the testator has ample opportunity of making their wishes known.

# Credit cards

The majority of banks issue their own Mastercard or Visa credit cards, which not only enable practitioners to make purchases by telephone or post, but allow a period of up to four weeks interest-free credit. They are, however, extremely costly in terms of interest if the bill is not paid promptly. The rates may be as much as 2% per month, which is an true rate of about 26.45% per annum, as it is compound interest.

However, such cards may be useful as a means of obtaining immediate payment from patients, particularly for private treatment, who might otherwise present payment problems. However, it is important to bear in mind that, as the trader, the dentist will have to pay a percentage (about 4%) of the money to the credit card company for its services and this ought to be built into the costs. There is also a registration fee of around £60.

American Express and Diners Club are both popular with dentists, particularly because of their value when travelling abroad, but also because of the loan privileges that they offer. It is, however, wise to bear in mind that they differ considerably from Mastercard and Visa in that payment is expected against the monthly statement. They are effectively 'charge cards', offering limited credit facilities.

## Other services

Banks today tend to offer a wide range of other services, ranging from use of night safes (often of little interest to the GDP) through to foreign currency dealings. The sensible practitioner will be acquainted with the various services, usually through the plethora of literature produced by the banks, and make their own decision as to which are likely to be of use professionally or privately.

# 8

# Insurance

All businesses need to have insurance cover and a dental practice is no exception. There is a wide range of cover available and usually this can be combined under a comprehensive trader's insurance policy. However, for present purposes the individual risks will be considered separately.

## Fire insurance

Generally this will cover the replacement of the asset covered, be it the freehold building or contents. An occupier of a leasehold premises will need to have insurance against loss of the property by fire, although this is usually effected by the landlord and the premium recharged to the tenant.

In the majority of cases, fire insurance of property is index-linked (ie the cover increases annually in line with increases in rebuilding costs) but it is essential to ensure that the starting base is correct otherwise the indexation is of doubtful value. The insurance needs to be in respect of reinstatement costs (which would obviously exclude the land) but the insured sum is likely to be considerably higher than the cost of the property. It would be sensible to take professional advice on the valuation at the outset.

Insurance of the contents must include also leased equipment, including the telephone, and should preferably be at replacement costs. It is wise to remember that most GDPs are constantly adding to or up-dating their equipment and at least a biannual review of the insurance values would be sensible.

It is also necessary to remember that adequate fire insurance is needed at home on building and contents. Where there is a mortgage, the building society will usually effect the insurance, although it might be appropriate to remember that one does not have to accept the building society insurers and it might be worthwhile seeking alternative quotations, particularly as some insurance companies base premiums solely on postcode areas.

## Comprehensive insurance

In many instances GDPs effect cover on their buildings extending beyond fire damage to include all other risks relating to the building and its fittings. It is prudent to have such cover as it will extend to storm damage and a host of other risks, including damage to fixed mirrors and sanitary ware, lost tiles from the roof, etc.

## All risks

An 'all risks' policy will cover the contents against damage from fire and extends to accidental damage through to, perhaps, dropping a piece of equipment accidentally. There are also 'all risks' policies to cover cameras, jewellery, etc.

## Public liability

Every business has a duty to protect visitors to their property against the consequences of an accident – a tile slipping off the roof, the visitor falling on a polished floor and so forth. Damages awarded by the Courts can be heavy, especially where a person is injured for life, and it is wise to check that adequate cover is held.

## Employer's liability

An employer must protect their staff against injury through accidents of whatever nature. In dentistry this can be especially important as many of the materials used in the surgery can be harmful, the instruments are sharp and there is a host of electrical equipment, often with (dangerously) trailing cables. This insurance will protect the employer against claims.

## Radiological accidents

The use of X-ray equipment in the surgery is in itself a serious risk and the GDP will need to insure against accidents to staff and patients alike through radiation. It is sensible to have an arrangement with the National Radiological Protection Board or similar organization, under which each employee will carry a badge that is sent regularly to be checked for exposure to radiation. It is also important that all radiological equipment is serviced regularly by a competent and qualified engineer.

## Pressure vessels insurance

Pressure vessels such as compressors, autoclaves and transportable gas containers, eg oxygen cylinders, should be regularly serviced and maintained to comply with current Health and Safety legislation (The Pressure System and Transportable Gas Container Regulation 1989).

## Burglary

Every business needs to insure against the consequences of breaking and entering, indeed there are some parts of large towns where it is virtually impossible to get insurance cover due to the high incidence of crime. Dental practices are often targets for the burglar who envisages an abundance of drugs, hypodermic needles and petty cash on the premises. Whilst the burglar may be disappointed, the damage caused in the break-in can be horrendous and it is clearly sensible to insure against such damage.

At home the practitioner will probably have goods susceptible to theft. These items all need adequate insurance.

## Consequential loss

A fire can be devastating, not only in terms of loss of the building and equipment but also in loss of business whilst the assets are reinstated. The effect of consequential loss is to ensure that the GDP has sufficient cover to meet the fixed outgoings whilst the insurers set about replacing the premises and contents. Indeed, there is the added point that, where an insurance company is committed to making a substantial weekly or monthly payment towards costs, this can act as a spur to prompt it into providing alternative facilities. It would be sensible to ensure that cover extends to loss of book debts due to destruction of the records, and also all professional charges (accountant, valuer, etc.).

# Money and book debts

Any member of staff who takes money to and from the bank will be vulnerable to theft and it is sensible to insure against both loss of the money itself and injury to the employee.

In the event of a fire destroying the accounting records, it would be beneficial to have insurance against outstanding book debts. It may be difficult to reconstruct the true claim but this will at least go some way towards making good the loss.

It is unlikely, however, that anyone in a dental practice can make economic insurance against bad debts arising, and this would hardly be worthwhile in any event, as the individual amounts outstanding would be comparatively small.

# Motor insurance

Every driver is required to have as a minimum third party insurance, which will make good damage caused to someone else (the third party) or their property. Most motorists will, however, have a fully comprehensive insurance, which will cover against repairs to the insured's own vehicle as well as that of the third party. A currently valid certificate of insurance is required before the vehicle can be taxed.

The insurance premium will vary depending on the make, age and value of the car, as well as on the location in which it is kept – some areas are more vulnerable to claims than others. The age of a driver will be pertinent because young people are regarded as a greater risk for the insurers.

A long period of no claim will be recompensed with a reduction in premium, which can also be increased by having a named driver and an excess on the policy. This means that the insured will bear an agreed portion of the risk. However, this does make it impossible for someone else to drive the vehicle in an emergency except under the third party cover of their own personal motor insurance. Whether this outweighs the saving in premium by having restricted cover is something only the policy holder can decide.

It would be sensible to check that the policy does have passenger insurance, particularly where the GDP may be carrying staff.

Holders of the Advanced Driving Test may often qualify for reduced premium on their motor insurance. Discounts may also be available on vehicles fitted with specific anti-theft devices, eg immobilizers.

# Permanent sickness

Anyone with regular commitments would be wise to ensure that they have adequate insurance to cover their outgoings in the event of sickness or accident disability. The premiums are fairly high and depend upon a combination of age, past medical record and amount of weekly cover. It may be that a reduction in the premium can be obtained by agreeing to delay the claim by one, three or six months.

Provided the policy is defined as permanent or non-cancellable, the insurance company is bound to renew it at the request of the policyholder without a fresh medical examination. Cover will usually be to the age of 60 or 65 years, but rarely beyond that age.

Any GDP should ensure that their associates have such cover so that there will be adequate funds to cover their commitments under the agreement. It might even be sensible to have this as a written condition in the associateship agreement.

# Professional negligence

The UK is rapidly being affected by the American trend of suing a professional for damages where negligence can be alleged. Sometimes such claims are unsuccessful but occasionally they do result in damages. Often such claims are for pain and suffering, failure to exercise a proper degree of skill and attention, for loss of earnings and perhaps medical treatment to recover lost instruments or similar.

Unlike most professionals, the GDP will usually be covered by membership of one of the Protection Societies. In the UK these will be either Dental Protection Ltd. (a division of the Medical Protection Society), the Medical Defence Union or the Medical Insurance Agency.

Where the practitioner is not so covered, it would be unwise to continue to operate without some form of insurance to cover the risk of having to pay damages.

# Professional fee protection

As will be seen later in this book, almost every GDP is liable to face an Inland Revenue investigation in the course of their career, and it would be prudent to insure against the professional costs involved in such an exercise. However, far too many practitioners fail to appreciate that the insurers are liable to exclude claims where the GDP has been lax in dealing with their accounts or income tax returns; and it is frequently the case that, all too late, the insured becomes aware that they are not really covered.

## General

The most important point the GDP needs to understand is that of averaging. Where a risk is under-insured the insurance company is likely to pay out only a proportion of any claim. Thus, a practitioner who has insured equipment for half of its real value cannot complain if the insurance company pays only half the value when a claim arises.

Another point that most practitioners fail to realize is that all insurance companies compare the claim form with the original proposal form. All too often there is a inclination, in making out a proposal form, to be somewhat economic with the truth on the basis that some items perhaps do not matter. When, however, it comes to making a claim, the insured will often become unusually truthful and will disclose information that ought to have been made known when the policy was effected; this can so easily invalidate a claim. The golden rule is to be extremely careful in filling in any proposal form, as well as when completing a claim form. It is also sensible to retain copies of all documentation.

It is a fact that it is possible to insure against almost any risk. If a commercial insurance company will not offer cover, it is likely that Lloyds of London will do so. Lloyds is an organisation of underwriters who will get together to cover risks, often of an unusual nature, but frequently the premium will be out of proportion to the benefit gained by the insurance and it would not be worthwhile buying cover. The future of Lloyds of London is currently uncertain and there may well be changes in the foreseeable future.

In the meantime, the nearest most GDPs will come to a Lloyds policy is in relation to a yacht.

## Life assurance

Dental surgeons, particularly around graduation time, are a target for insurance brokers seeking to sell life assurance. All too often the young graduates are sold cover that is not suitable to their needs.

There is a whole range of different life policies on the market, many of which can be adapted to different needs. Basically there are two kinds of life assurance:

1 Whole life, where the sum assured is paid out only on the death of the assured.
2 Endowment, where the sum assured is paid out either on death or at a predetermined date, whichever is the earlier.

In both cases the sum assured may be with profits or not. If it is, then the policyholder will participate in the profits made by the insurance company; in other cases they will not. If the insurance company is a mutual society, the whole of the profits go back to the policyholders; in a proprietary company the shareholders share in the profits of the company. It follows that the best sort of policy is the with-profits endowment assurance but this is, of course, more expensive. The least costly is the straightforward whole life cover.

Insurance for school fees insurance and inheritance tax policies are variations on these themes. Under the former, there is usually a series of policies that mature at annual intervals, giving money towards the school fees (as it is difficult to predict the growth in education costs in advance, the insurance is often not sufficient by itself). With the latter type of policy, the benefit of the policy is assigned to the beneficiaries to form a separate estate and the amount of cover is designed to provide funds to meet the inheritance tax.

There are, of course, other variations depending on individual circumstances. In relation to life assurance, it is perhaps sensible to bear in mind:

1 The average young practitioner probably does not have any specific need for life assurance because they probably do not have any dependents. In such cases it is sensible to look at life assurance as a means of saving, and endowment assurance over, say, the minimum period of ten years is sufficient.
2 On marriage the GDP will need life assurance in some form, but it is wise not to over-commit because if a family follows, this means additional domestic expenses, which have a first claim on the GDP's income.
3 Far too many young dentists are persuaded to take out life assurance (or pension policies) to a degree that will cause financial strain in later life when they take on a mortgage and have a family. This can also lead to the sort of financial difficulties that are so prevalent in dental practices and that result in practitioners having to continually re-mortgage their properties to release the equity.
4 Always remember that it does not pay to surrender or otherwise disturb a policy once it is in force. Most surrender values are less than the total premiums paid to date.

5    The golden rule is to be certain that your life cover is adequate, appropriate and manageable. Do not take on more than you can control whatever the reasons put to you. A good insurance broker will keep the situation under constant review and will give the same advice.

# Endowment and pension mortgages

The majority of building societies and banks are keen that borrowers should have this type of mortgage. Only the interest is paid by the borrower and the capital sum is provided by the tax-free lump sum paid on maturity. The idea is sound but there are factors which need to be borne in mind.

1    Usually this form of mortgage is rather more costly to the young practitioner than a repayment mortgage. This is because the loan remains unchanged and consequently the full interest continues to be paid alongside the endowment or pension premium. To some extent, however, the Inland Revenue is effectively contributing towards the ultimate capital repayment from the lump sum as well as the tax relief on the annual interest (subject to statutory restrictions).
2    There has been much discussion as to whether the lump sum should be taxed. If it is to be subject to tax, particularly at the higher band, the amount available for clearing the mortgage will possibly be insufficient to cover the outstanding debt. Whether any taxing legislation will be retrospective would be a very material point, so far there has been little retrospective  fiscal legislation, but that does not debar it.
3    It would perhaps be sensible to obtain independent advice  before taking out such a mortgage in case the question of commission is colouring the judgement of the lender.

# Low-start mortgages

In recent years many GDPs have been attracted by this type of mortgage, under which a low rate of interest is charged in the early years and the difference rolled up to increase later repayments. All too often the borrower comes to regret the decision to take up such a mortgage because they have tended to encourage dentists to over-stretch themselves and, by the time the full interest has become payable, income has not increased in proportion.

# 9

# Book-keeping

In the past, GDPs have regarded themselves as professionals working in a highly paid profession. They have not been prepared to accept that they are working in a business that has to be profitable in order to survive. Indeed, it is only in the past five years that this realism has been accepted. As with any business, the dentist will need to maintain at least some basic accounting records which will:

1    Accurately record all income and its sources.
2    Accurately record all expenditure including the principal's drawings.
3    Keep track of the assets and liabilities.

Unfortunately, GDPs are notoriously bad at maintaining even the simplest of records (other than their clinical records) and seem unwilling, in the majority of cases, to employ a competent book-keeper. Indeed, where any sort of books are maintained, this is left to either the receptionist or to the dentist's spouse, neither of whom may have adequate training.

More often the practitioner delivers a box of assorted and muddled paperwork to an accountant (frequently with essential papers missing) and expects accounts to be prepared from such chaos economically.

The maintenance of good records will have many benefits including:

1    Keeping accountancy charges at a reasonable level.
2    Giving the GDP the information necessary to make decisions and to have proper control over the finances and practice.
3    Minimising the risk of problems if the Inland Revenue conducts an investigation, either into the accounts or a wages audit.
4    Greatly reducing the risk of fraud within the practice because staff who see the principal operating slipshod methods with inadequate control over cash, may be tempted to stray from the right path and to dip their hands into the till.

Indeed, it is often only when the practitioner has experienced the professional cost and trauma and penalties of an Inland Revenue investigation that they can be persuaded to keep adequate records.

# Income

The income of a dental practice will usually derive from a variety of sources:

1   Patients' NHS contributions (which today represents a fairly large proportion of overall income).
2   Private fees for dental treatment.
3   Remittances from the DPB for NHS treatment including child entry payments, child capitation, adult continuing care, and item of service payments.
4   Remittances from dental health schemes.
5   Sale of dental requisites, toothbrushes, floss, etc.
6   Reimbursement of vocational trainee salaries.
7   Other items (eg sale of equipment or scrap metal such as gold and amalgam).

As the Inspector of Taxes will assume that cash can easily go astray, the GDP will be expected to maintain a careful record of all monies coming into the practice. It is frequently here that the problems begin because the GDP assumes that sufficient data is given on the payment schedules for preparation of the accounts or that a summary of bankings is sufficient. It is the dearth of records at this point which causes the greatest problems for the accountant trying to produce accurate accounts.

The sensible practitioner will have a counter-book, maintained by the receptionist, which records all income, irrespective of its source (Figure 9.1). This book needs to be balanced daily against the cash banked and cash in the till. Under no circumstances should money be removed from the till, for whatever reason. If this is made a rule and the staff are required to adhere to it, there should be an adequate control over monies flowing into the practice that will stand scrutiny by an Inspector of Taxes or anyone else.

Any differences revealed by the counter-book ought to be investigated and explained. With such a system in operation, any theft would be minimized and, where it does take place, there would be sufficient evidence to identify such losses.

The counter-book should be checked periodically against the surgery day-book or appointment book to ensure that the associates are not taking cash in the surgery and by-passing the receptionist. It should also be checked against receipt books to ensure that no money covered by a receipt has been omitted from the counter-book.

Every surgery should also maintain a register of forms sent to the DPB for payment and steps should be taken to ensure that fees are eventually received. Apart from, again, acting as a check on the DPB, this does enable the current debtors to be established at any particular point in time.

COUNTERBOOK

| Date 1992 | Name | Receipt No | Total Received | PRINCIPAL | | | ASSOCIATE | | | Sundry Sales | Other Receipts |
|---|---|---|---|---|---|---|---|---|---|---|---|
| | | | | NHS Fees | Private Fees | Dental Health | NHS Fees | Private Fees | Dental Health | | |
| 1-5 | Patient Charges | 1-11 | 172.50 | 97.50 | | | 75.00 | | | | |
| 2-5 | Fees | 12-20 | 301.00 | | 205.00 | | | 96.00 | | | |
| 3-5 | Patient charges | 21-33 | 256.30 | 130.00 | 126.30 | | | | | | |
| 4-5 | Patient charges | 34-40 | 498.50 | 100.00 | 49.50 | | 100.00 | 249.00 | | | |
| 5-5 | Denplan | | 471.72 | | | 271.72 | | | 200.00 | | |
| 5-5 | Patient charges 2 TOOTHBRUSHES | 41-56 | 530.00 | 94.00 | 198.00 | | 120.00 | 105.00 | | 13.00 | |
| 8-5 | D.P.B | | 5398.00 | 3597.71 | | | 1800.29 | | | | |
| 8-5 | Sale of Typewriter | 57 | 50.00 | | | | | | | | 50.00 |
| | | | 7678.02 | 4019.21 | 578.80 | 271.72 | 2095.29 | 450.00 | 200.00 | 13.00 | 50.00 |
| | | | | | | | | | | | |

Figure 9.1   Counter Book

The receipt books should be retained with counterfoils completed and a file kept in reception containing all the back-up paperwork to verify the practice income.

In some practices the counter-book will be replaced with an electronic, till which issues numbered receipts and analyses the income mechanically. That is an excellent substitute for the manual record, provided the till rolls are carefully dated and preserved for future reference.

The collection of records should be adequate in any dental practice and, whilst it may take time to complete, the benefits will be considerable.

## Petty cash

The only other monies that need to be handled through reception are petty cash payments. This is yet another weak area in many practices; either the GDP will give the DSA money from their own pocket to make small purchases (and then often forget what has been done, or lose the receipt) or the money will be taken out of patients' fee income and, again, frequently not recorded.

At the end of the year it is then necessary to make an educated guess at what has been spent, and this is yet another area in which the Inspector of Taxes will see the opportunity for evasion of tax.

A properly kept petty cash book will prove invaluable provided it is balanced regularly and any shortfall in cash explained at the time. Indeed, it is best if the petty cash is maintained on the imprest system under which the receptionist is given a specific float, which is topped up at intervals by reimbursing the expenditure incurred. Thus, at any time the float should be represented either by cash in the petty cash box or by receipts for payments awaiting reimbursement. The funds should be replenished from the bank and not from the patients' fees or the GDP's own pocket.

The records in the reception desk should be made up contemporaneously and balanced properly at the end of the day. Thus, the GDP can be sure that all funds flowing into the surgery, and thence into the practice bank account, are being properly controlled.

PETTY CASH BOOK

| Income | Date | Details | Total | Materials | Wages | Canteen | Postage | Travel | Cleaning | Stat | Sundries |
|--------|------|---------|-------|-----------|-------|---------|---------|--------|----------|------|----------|
| | 1-5 | Coffee | 1·69 | | | 1·69 | | | | | |
| | 2-5 | Postage Stamps | 3·60 | | | | 3·60 | | | | |
| | 3-5 | Milk | 6·84 | | | 6·84 | | | | | |
| | 4-5 | Light Bulbs | 3·60 | | | | | | | | 3·60 |
| 30·00 | 5-5 | from Bank | | | | | | | | | |
| | 5-5 | Train Fare - Course | 12·60 | | | | | 12·60 | | | |
| | 5-5 | Else - cleaner | 10·00 | | | | | | 10·00 | | |
| | 5-5 | Chemist - C…… | 1·21 | 1·21 | | | | | | | |
| 30·00 | | | 39·54 | 1·21 | | 8·53 | 3·60 | 12·60 | 10·00 | | 3·60 |
| | | Balance b/fwd | 36·50 | | | | | | | | |
| | | Income | 30·00 | | | | | | | | |
| | | | 66·50 | | | | | | | | |
| | | Expenditure | 39·54 | | | | | | | | |
| | | Balance c/fwd | 26·96 | Agreed to Cash box. | | | | | | | |

Figure 9.2   Petty Cash Book

Cash book – Income

| Date | Details | Cash | Bank | PRINCIPAL | | ASSOCIATE | | Sundry Sales | Contra | Other |
|---|---|---|---|---|---|---|---|---|---|---|
| | | | | NHS | Private | NHS | Private | | | |
| 4/6 | Bankings | | 729.80 | 227.50 | 331.30 | 75.00 | 96.00 | | | |
| 5/6 | Denplan | | 471.72 | | 271.72 | | 200.00 | | | |
| 8/6 | D.P.B. | | 5398.00 | 3597.71 | | 1800.29 | | | | |
| 8/6 | Bankings | | 1078.50 | 194.00 | 247.50 | 220.00 | 354.00 | 13.00 | | 50.00 |
| | | | 7678.02 | 4019.21 | 850.52 | 2095.29 | 650.00 | 13.00 | | 50.00 |
| | Balance b/fwd | 546.02 | | | Agrees to bank statement | | | | | |
| | Receipts | 7678.02 | | | | | | | | |
| | | 8224.04 | | | | | | | | |
| | Payments | 6752.47 | | | | | | | | |
| | Balance c/fwd | 1471.57 | | | | | | | | |

Figure 9.3    Petty Cash Book – Income Section

Cash book – Expenditure 1992

| Date June | Details | Chq. no. | Cash | Bank | Materials | Technician | Hygienist | Associate | Equipment Lease | Staff Salaries | Rent & Rates | Heat & Light | Post/Phone Stat. | Motor Expenses | Sundries | Capital | Personal |
|---|---|---|---|---|---|---|---|---|---|---|---|---|---|---|---|---|---|
| 2nd | Telephone | 250 | | 157.45 | | | | | | | | | 157.45 | | | | |
| 3rd | Insurance | 251 | | 186.50 | | | | | | | | | | | Aratue 186.50 | | |
| 4th | ABC Supplies | 252 | | 356.02 | 356.02 | | | | | | | | | | | | |
| 5th | Wages-Recep | 253 | | 110.40 | | | | | | 110.40 | | | | | | | |
| 8th | Labs. | 254 | | 1200.00 | | 1200.00 | | | | | | | | | | | |
| 15th | Equip. Lease D/D | D/D | | 123.50 | | | | | 123.50 | | | | | | | | |
| 15th | Rates D/D | D/D | | 247.30 | | | | | | | 247.30 | | | | | | |
| 19th | Electricity | 255 | | 120.80 | | | | | | | | 120.80 | | | | | |
| 25th | Petrol AK | 256 | | 156.00 | | | | | | | | | | 156.00 | | | |
| 26th | LG Equip. | 257 | | 350.00 | | | | | | | | | | | | Don barnet 350.00 | |
| 30th | Miss Clean | 258 | | 247.50 | | | 247.50 | | | | | | | | | | |
| 30th | A. Smith | 259 | | 1800.00 | | | | 1800.00 | | | | | | | | | |
| 30th | Wages Giro | | | 1697.00 | | | | | | 1697.00 | | | | | | | |
| | | | | 6752.47 | 356.02 | 1200.00 | 247.50 | 1800.00 | 123.50 | 1807.40 | 247.30 | 120.80 | 157.45 | 156.00 | 186.50 | 350.00 | |

Figure 9.4   Petty Cash Book – Expenditure Section

# Main cash book

This book will usually be kept by the book-keeper and will bring together all the other records. Usually it is best divided into two separate sections:

1    Income (Figure 9.3).
2    Expenditure (Figure 9.4).

This will usually cover all the monies paid into the bank and the cheques issued.

It will be seen that these books can contain a record of cash received and not banked, and of cash payments made, although the use of cash is not to be recommended. It is usually better to bank all cash intact and to make payments by cheque because, apart from any other consideration, this does ensure a permanent record and challenges any criticism by the Inspector of Taxes.

The GDP will also be well advised to ensure that all receipts and other documentation is filed away carefully in the order it appears in the cash book because that will ensure it can be easily checked.

# Salaries and wages

A salary is usually based on an annual rate of pay, even though paid monthly; it is not usual to pay overtime to a salary earner. On the other hand, wages are normally paid hourly and will rank for overtime payment.

In some instances the payroll is handled by an outside agency, in which case it will provide the payslips and a schedule of the amounts to be paid to the employees. The tax and national insurance records will be retained by the agency, which will also cope with the sick and maternity pay as well as the year-end returns.

Where the records are maintained internally within the practice it is sensible to maintain a wages book, but each employee should receive a payslip.

The net pay should correspond with the entry in the cash book; and there should be a statement showing the composition of payments remitted to the Inland Revenue in respect of tax and national insurance deductions, adjusted as appropriate for SSP or SMP (Figure 9.5).

| Tax Remitted on 17th July 1993. | | |
|---|---|---|
| Deducted from  Miss Smith | | 119 ·84 |
| Mr. Jones | | 121 ·14 |
| Mrs Burton | | 45·72 |
| | | |
| NHI for  Miss Smith | | 27·39 |
| Mr. Jones | | 28·01 |
| Mrs. Burton | | 7·30 |
| | | |
| | | 349 ·40 |
| Less  SSP | 19 ·04 | |
| SMP | — | 19 ·04 |
| Net Remittance | | 330·36 |

Figure 9.5    Statement

# 10

# Cash flow statements and budgets

In recent years banks and finance houses have placed a great deal of emphasis on seeing forecasts when considering loan applications or reviewing credit limits. The majority of GDPs regard this as an imposition, particularly as they feel it necessary to involve their accountant in preparation of these documents, which they perceive as useless. In reality, provided the practice maintains a good set of accounting records (along the lines suggested in Chapter 9) the preparation of the cash projection – often called a cash flow statement – is not a difficult task. Indeed, it can be a useful tool for management of a practice because it will highlight where cash problems are likely to occur and indicate how they can be resolved in advance. A yachtsman would hardly set sail in unfamiliar waters without some sort of chart; but the same individuals are quite content often to run their dental practices with little idea of where they have been nor whence they are bound, beyond the general view that they seek to maximize profitability.

## Budgets

The starting point for any cash projection is a budget of earnings, and initial efforts at producing one will doubtless be inaccurate although, with some practice, it is possible to become quite efficient at the task.

Example: A GDP has been in practice for several years and his gross fee income for the last financial year amounted to £257,986. An examination of the accounting records shows that this was earned from NHS work (76%) and private patients (24%) It also discloses that 56% of all fees were earned by the principal and the remaining 44% by the associate.

|  | Private | NHS | Total |
|---|---|---|---|
| Principal | £ 86,271 | £109,799 | £196,070 |
| Associate | £ 14,860 | £ 47,056 | £ 61,916 |
|  | £101,131 | £156,855 | £257,986 |

It is now necessary to consider the next accounting year and the type of work to be undertaken. Assume that the principal has decided to go wholly private, which will inevitably mean a loss of patients (experience has shown this is likely to be of the order of 21% but will be fully compensated by increased fees). The associate, who remains an NHS dentist, may have to forego about 10% of private patients to take up the additional NHS workload. This means that the next year, taking into account a 5% fee increase in NHS work, could be expected to realize the following fees:

|  | Private | NHS | Total |
|---|---|---|---|
| Principal | £196,070 |  | £196,070 |
| Associate | £ 24,520 | £55,427 | £ 79,947 |
|  | £220,590 | £55,427 | £276,017 |

The principal's fee income should remain the same because although 21% of NHS patients have been lost, the fees from the remainder are higher. The associate's private work has fallen by 10% but 21% of the principal's NHS patients have come to the associate (£18,117) and this, along with the associate's own NHS patients (£34,672) gives a total of £52,789, which will have increased by 5% to £55,427.

The next point to consider is the spread over the year. If the bulk of the principal's work (usually 72%) comes from a dental health scheme, it will be spread evenly despite holidays. However, the remaining 28% will probably be earned erratically, although this is open to conjecture. The associate will have a 'core' of continuing care along with erratic monthly schedules:

|  | Principal | Associate | Total |
|---|---|---|---|
| May | £14,784 | £8,299 | £23,083 |
| June | £13,648 | £7,948 | £21,596 |
| July | £15,922 | £8,226 | £24,148 |
| August | £20,113 | £7,884 | £27,997 |
| September | £11,764 | £7,862 | £19,626 |
| October | £17,994 | £8,911 | £26,905 |
| November | £18,420 | £6,783 | £25,203 |
| December | £20,426 | £1,440 | £21,866 |
| January | £13,228 | £9,114 | £22,342 |
| February | £14,889 | £8,229 | £23,118 |
| March | £18,222 | £8,916 | £27,138 |
| April | £31,444 | £4,643 | £36,078 |

This includes a basic capitation for the principal of £11,764 per month. The associate will have continuing care of £1,440 per month. Thus we have the income profile for the next twelve months.

## Direct costs

The direct costs of the practice can be assessed at a percentage of gross fee income by examining the last annual accounts:

| Materials | 7% (national average between 5% and 7%). |
|---|---|
| Technician | 14% (national average between 12% and 18%). |
| Salaries (except reception, etc.) | 11% (national average between 9% and 17%). |
| Equipment maintenance | 1% (national average between 1% and 4%). |

The associate is paid 50% after deduction of laboratory bills. The associate is usually paid when the schedule is received from the FHSA. Salaries must, of course, be paid contemporaneously (for the sake of simplicity tax has been treated as 'set aside' at the point the salaries are paid although usually there will be a one month credit period). All other expenditure is paid after thirty days.

Thus, we now have a working budget, which can be converted into a monthly pattern of income and expenditure with no major difficulty:

| | | | |
|---|---|---|---|
| Fee income | | £276,017 | 100% |
| Materials | £19,321 | | 7% |
| Technician | £38,642 | | 14% |
| Associate | £34,377 | | * |
| Salaries | £30,362 | | 11% |
| Equipment repair | £2,760 | | 1% |
| Establishment costs | £11,040 | | 4% |
| Administration | £41,403 | | 15% |
| | ———— | | |
| Expenses | £177,906 | | |
| Net profit | | £98,111 | 35% |

\* £79,947 less 14% laboratory bill × 50%

# Cash projections

Once the budget has been prepared, it is a simple matter to produce the cash projection by inserting the data on a pro forma, which classifies the income and expenditure by months. Allowing for time lag in receipt of payment of cash, it is possible to ascertain the cash expected to flow into and out of the practice on a monthly basis and, consequently, the net in- or outflow. By adjusting this on the bank balance at the beginning of the month it is possible to estimate how the balance should stand at the end of the month.

Where there is a shortfall (or overdraft) one can see if it is likely to exceed the authorized bank borrowing limit. If so, the situation can be remedied by holding over payment of some bills until the situation improves or, perhaps less attractively, arranging with the bank to have an increased borrowing limit for a short period.

It will be noted that provision has been made in the cash projection for personal drawings as well as for mortgage interest. These monies will need to be found each month.

The sensible GDP will prepare the budget and cash projection not simply to keep the bank manager quiet, but also for management purposes.

It will also be monitored on a regular basis. This can be achieved by having a blank column alongside each month and entering the actual income and expenditure each month, so that comparison with the projection is achieved. This will be a sound discipline, forcing the GDP to keep a regular watch on the practice, and will also greatly improve the quality and accuracy of budgeting over a period of time.

NAME:

## INCOME

| | May '93 | Jun '93 | Jul '93 | Aug '93 | Sept '93 | Oct '93 | Nov '93 | Dec '93 | Jan '94 | Feb '94 | Mar '94 | Apr '94 | Total |
|---|---|---|---|---|---|---|---|---|---|---|---|---|---|
| FEES  –Principal | 14784 | 13648 | 15922 | 20113 | 11764 | 17994 | 18420 | 20426 | 13228 | 14889 | 18222 | 31444 | 210854 |
| –Associate | 8299 | 7948 | 8226 | 7884 | 7862 | 8911 | 6783 | 1440 | 9114 | 8229 | 8916 | 4634 | 88246 |
| | 23083 | 21596 | 24148 | 27997 | 19626 | 26905 | 25203 | 21866 | 22342 | 23118 | 27138 | 36078 | 299100 |
| **EXPENDITURE** | | | | | | | | | | | | | |
| Materials | 1616 | 1512 | 1690 | 1960 | 1374 | 1883 | 1764 | 1531 | 1564 | 1618 | 1899 | 2525 | 20936 |
| Technicians | 3232 | 3023 | 3381 | 3920 | 2748 | 3717 | 3528 | 3061 | 3128 | 3237 | 3799 | 5051 | 41825 |
| Wages and NI | 2376 | 2656 | 3080 | 2159 | 2960 | 2772 | 2405 | 2458 | 2543 | 2985 | 3969 | | 30363 |
| Associate | 3538 | 3418 | 3537 | 3390 | 3381 | 3832 | 2917 | 619 | 3919 | 3538 | 3834 | 1993 | 37916 |
| Equipment Maintenance | 231 | 216 | 242 | 280 | 196 | 269 | 252 | 219 | 233 | 231 | 271 | 361 | 3001 |
| Establishment Expenses | 594 | 864 | 965 | 1120 | 785 | 1077 | 1008 | 875 | 893 | 925 | 1085 | 1443 | 11634 |
| Administration | 3231 | 3033 | 3380 | 3920 | 2747 | 3767 | 3528 | 3062 | 3127 | 3237 | 3799 | 5051 | 41882 |
| Drawings | 2000 | 2000 | 2000 | 2000 | 2000 | 2000 | 2000 | 2000 | 2000 | 2000 | 2000 | 2000 | 24000 |
| | 16818 | 16722 | 18275 | 18749 | 16191 | 19317 | 17402 | 13825 | 17407 | 17771 | 20656 | 18424 | 211557 |
| **BANK BALANCE** | | | | | | | | | | | | | |
| Brought Forward | 482 | 6978 | 12068 | 18133 | 27661 | 31292 | 39149 | 47202 | 55462 | 60630 | 66208 | 72961 | 482 |
| Plus Receipts | 23083 | 21596 | 24148 | 27997 | 19626 | 26905 | 25203 | 21866 | 22342 | 23118 | 27138 | 36078 | 299100 |
| Less Payments | 16587 | 16506 | 18033 | 18469 | 15995 | 19048 | 17150 | 13606 | 17174 | 17540 | 20385 | 18063 | 211557 |
| Carried Forward | 6978 | 12068 | 18183 | 27661 | 31292 | 39149 | 47202 | 55462 | 60630 | 66208 | 72961 | 90976 | 88025 |

**Figure 10.1** Cash Flow Projection

## Private fee income

One side-benefit to this sort of exercise is the ability to determine an accurate rate for fees in respect of private work.

Even in the hey day of NHS dentistry it was not unusual for some patients to demand private treatment whilst, in other cases, the dentist perhaps felt that there were procedures (eg the provision of dentures) that could not be untaken profitably other than on a fee-paying basis.

In most instances the GDP will fix a fee scale by reference to individual circumstances, on the basis of rates charged by competitors or as recommended by organisations such as CODE. Others simply take the NHS scales and add some arbitrary percentage. These practices do show a profit but it is questionable whether they truly reflected the GDP's own situation.

All private fees should be fixed individually for each dentist; the preparation of a budget allows for this.

The starting point here is the sum that the practitioner considers is a fair return for the effort and the hours they are prepared to work to achieve that objective, ie the amount the GDP wishes to earn.

Example: If we assume that the practitioner has set his target income at £50,000 before tax; and is prepared to work for four days, leaving one day free for paperwork. The surgery will be operating from 9 a.m. until 1 p.m. and from 2 p.m. until 5 p.m. during the working days.

The practitioner will have a working week of 4 × 7 hours = 28 hours. Allowing for four weeks holiday and the usual bank holidays, as well as a provision of three weeks for illness, there will be an available working period of (52 weeks less (4 for holidays, 2 for bank holidays and 3 for sickness)) = 43 weeks at 28 hours = 1204 hours. However, no-one is 100% efficient; studies have shown that 70% efficiency is the maximum but 60% more likely. This will reduce the working hours to 722.5. To earn £50,000 in that period will necessitate a charge of £69.20 per hour, say £70. Still it is necessary to recover certain costs:

| | |
|---|---|
| DSA salaries | 11% |
| Equipment maintenance | 1% |
| Establishment costs | 4% |
| Administration costs | 15% |

To ensure these are covered it is necessary to increase the hourly rate to:

£70 × (100 ÷ 100 − 31) = £101

This does not, of course, take into account dental materials or laboratory charges. If these are to be included too (7% materials and 14% laboratory charges), the rate will have to be increased still further to:

£101 × (100 ÷ 100 − 21) = £128.

It is essential that the dentist has this information readily available when quoting fees, but it will still be necessary to estimate the amount of time that any procedure is likely to take, which is, of course, something that will differ materially from one practitioner to another.

Certainly, it would be prudent when quoting fees to ensure that the patient fully understands the eventual costs. Many disputes could have been avoided by stating the fee in writing, with any possible variations.

Some capitation-based dental health schemes require the patient to pay the laboratory charge in addition to the monthly capitation payment, which is expected to cover everything else. If this is the case the hourly charge in the above example should be £101 × (100 ÷ 100 − 4) = £105.

# 11

# Computers in dentistry

When the personal computer (PC) became more accessible, people from all walks of life rushed to acquire their computer before deciding why it was needed or what they intended to do with it. Many GDPs acquired machines and used them to produce their accounts or payrolls.

Over the ensuing years there has become a greater awareness of the value of the computer and machines on the market have not only become more powerful but specialist programmes have been written for them. Today we are rapidly reaching the stage when the computer is becoming an essential tool for good management and it is perhaps the time to seriously consider acquiring such equipment.

## Applications

The main uses of a computer in a dental practice are:

1   Maintaining an appointment system, particularly where there are several practitioners working on the same premises.
2   Issue of recalls, which will maintain a steady throughput of patients.
3   Issue of reminders for account payments.
4   Word processing.
5   Maintenance of accounts, provided a suitable programme is used (and here it is recommended that the GDP should not set up a system without prior consultation with an accountant to ensure that it meets the requirements of the practice adequately).
6   Preparation of the payroll, provided the programme is suitable. However, it is unlikely that this would prove beneficial for a payroll of less than twelve people.
7   Maintenance of clinical records. Apart from needing a suitable programme, it is wise to bear in mind that there could be legal problems. Where a negligence claim comes before the Courts, any manuscript clinical records would clearly show any alterations; seldom would a computer record do so, and it is conceivable that the Court might be inclined to give the benefit of any doubt to the patient in such a situation. This is something which has yet to be decided in the

Courts but, in the absence of precedent, care should be exercised before moving to computerized clinical records. There is also the problem that, on a multi-terminal system, precautions need to be taken against loss of data through a programme crash.

8 Transfer of data to the DPB. For a practitioner working within the NHS system, swift transfer of data to the Board will often expedite payment of fees. However, any such system needs to be introduced with care to avoid problems over inaccurate claims and their consequences. The DPB encourages EDI (electronic data interchange) and offers an incentive grant which is payable after the first successful transmission.

9 Banking. It is now possible to operate a bank account through a computer system using a modem and telephone line.

Inevitably some GDPs are more technology literate and will adapt to the use of computers more quickly than others. There is no doubt that such tools are useful provided the practitioner has decided in advance the use to which the equipment will be put, has decided that it is cost-effective and has taken every precaution to ensure both that the program is the right one for that practice and that there are adequate precautions against potential problems.

## Training

A sensible practitioner will ensure that all staff attend suitable training courses to understand and to operate the system correctly and effectively. Practitioners should be able to operate the system themselves.

## Decisions about hardware and software

It would be wise to carry out proper research before buying any hardware or software. Research avoids the expensive mistakes that result from buying one or both and then finding that they are incompatible or inappropriate to the requirements of the practice. As salesmen are inevitably enthusiastic about their products, they are probably not the best judge of what is needed. It is far better to speak to a colleague who has a system in operation and to see it working in the everyday environment. Discussion with the operator will reveal the problems which have been observed and how they were resolved.

Alternatively there are companies that specialize in advising on suitable equipment and programmes, although it is sensible to ensure that they do understand the peculiarities of the dental profession.

## Lease versus purchase

Whether the equipment is leased or purchased is a question of personal choice in most instances. The tax position is discussed elsewhere in this book. However, many GDPs feel they will have a greater protection and opportunity to replace the hardware if it is leased.

## Electronic processing of NHS claims

From April 1991, following a pilot scheme, the GDP can have a computer system that will electronically transmit claims from the surgery computer via a telephone line to the DPB. They are processed overnight so that the payment tapes can be forwarded monthly to the bank in order to credit the funds to the practitioner's bank. The advantage to both parties is the reduction in paperwork, swifter clearance of queries and prior approval applications, reduction of error and a quicker turn-round of payment. Systems on sale to the profession have to submit to certification by the DPB after stringent tests. It is anticipated that within five years the majority of dental practices working within the NHS will be linked to the DPB and use the EDI (electronic data interchange) facility.

## Advantages of computerisation

1   A more efficient appointment register with automatic recalls and reminders.
2   Improved patient billing and debt collection with a consequent improvement in cash flow and financial management.
3   Improved book-keeping, stock control and correspondence (using the word processing facility).

   Whether or not it is sensible to replace the manual account books with the computer is questionable. Apart  from the fact that the volume of work probably does not justify computerisation, there is also the point that anyone keeping manual records is likely to be in closer touch with transactions.

# 12

# Sole practitioners and partnerships

## Sole practitioners

Many GDPs are sole practitioners, and this has the distinct advantage of being able to make all the decisions without recourse to anyone else. Indeed, it is this freedom that causes many to remain in this position, although undoubtedly it may be necessary to engage an associate or hygienist to assist with the clinical work. However, it is probable that the disadvantages are likely to outweigh the benefits:

1   There is no other clinician to consult when difficulties arise in the dental work. Associates are likely to be less experienced than the principal; older GDPs with more experience would probably have moved on to become principals themselves.
2   All finance has to be provided by one individual, whether it be the working capital or monies to acquire further equipment or premises.
3   As all the decisions fall to one individual, they will need to be experienced not only in dentistry but also in all other aspects of business management, ie accountancy, sales, staff control, purchasing, etc.
4   In the event of illness, holidays or educational courses, there is usually no one to take over care of the patients.
5   Where an associate is employed, the fear of their resignation is likely to add to the GDP's worries.

## Partnership

The Partnership Act (1890) defines a partnership as 'an association of two or more persons trading together with a view to a profit', which means that they share the net profit in some predetermined ratio. It is not essential that there should be anything in writing but, in that event the remaining provisions of the Partnership Act (1890) will apply – profits and losses to be shared equally and all capital to be provided in the same proportion. Where any one individual provides capital in excess of that invested by the others the difference will be treated as a loan, bearing interest at 5% per annum.

If it is thought best to deviate from these arrangements it is essential that there should be a written document varying the terms, for example to enable profits and losses to be shared in a different ratio. The documentation need only be an exchange of letters and not necessarily a formal written partnership agreement, although it would be exceedingly unwise not to have one.

The main provisions in a partnership agreement are:

1   Date of commencement and duration if it is to be for a fixed period.
2   Identification of the parties.
3   Profit sharing (and, if appropriate, salary) arrangements.
4   Duties of the individual partners.
5   Arrangements for banking, book-keeping and preparation of annual accounts.
6   Holiday and sickness arrangements.
7   Provision for terminating the arrangement, either on a voluntary basis or forcibly in the event of bankruptcy or death.
8   Valuation of the assets for dissolution.
9   Usually arbitration provisions for settlement of any dispute between the parties.
10  Arrangements for paying off the outgoing partner or his dependants.

In the UK the average life of the traditional partnership is about twelve months, although it is sometimes longer in the dental profession. Even so, unrest stems from unequal sharing of effort and profit. Nevertheless, the life is finite and the association is liable to culminate in a dispute and dissolution. Such a situation can be both costly and traumatic and it is often only some months later that the real cost is apparent.

The Inland Revenue can often take two or three years to finalize the tax liability of a partnership, by which time the parties have gone their own way. It is then (or in the case of a bankruptcy) that the remaining GDP will realize that a partnership has the disadvantage of joint and several liability. This means that the creditors can look to the partners together or individually for the whole of the partnership liabilities, including tax or bank overdraft. The remaining partner can then find that they have to pay off the former partner's tax or share of the bank borrowing. This will frequently cause hardship and distress.

# Expense-sharing partnerships

It was to overcome this problem that the dental profession has evolved the 'expense-sharing' partnership. This is really something of a misnomer because it is nothing more than an association of two or more independent practitioners working together on the same premises and sharing the expenses. Usually, each practitioner will own a share in the freehold or lease and the furnishings and equipment of the common parts of the surgery (eg the central sterilising room, the panoral X-ray, the waiting room and reception, etc.). They will also own the equipment in their own individual surgery (including the hand instruments).

Apart from the technicians' charges and any specifically personal expenditure (such as motor expenses and professional subscriptions) all expenses will be met jointly from a common pool into which the participants contribute on a monthly basis or similar.

In most cases the contribution will be worked out in proportion to gross fee income for the period, subject to a minimum and maximum share to take into account the cases in which any one of the practitioners is off work and his colleague(s) might otherwise have to bear all the expenses for that period.

Example: Brown and Green are expense-sharing practitioners who have agreed to a minimum monthly contribution of £2000 and a maximum of £4000. The expenses for the month amounted to £5000 and the division is according to gross fee income. Brown earned fees of £8000 and Green of £2000. The contributions would be:

Brown: £8000 ÷ £10,000 = 80% of £5000 = £4000

Green: £2000 ÷ £10000 = 20% of £5000 + £1000 = £2000

But the minimum contribution is £2000 which means that the division would be:

Brown: £5000 less Green's minimum of £2000 = £3000

Green: minimum contribution = £2000

Of course, the existence of an expense-sharing arrangement will not prevent a break-up but it does have certain advantages over a traditional partnership:

1   The joint and several liability concept does not apply and consequently one 'partner' cannot be left to face debts incurred by the other.

2    The commencement and cessation provisions in tax law do not apply because there can be no partnership change at any stage; each GDP operates their own individual practice.
3    There are no requirements that one 'partner' should buy out the retiring one. It may be prudent to do so in order to prevent a newcomer who is unacceptable, but this is a question of choice only.

However, it is necessary to enter into such an arrangement with some care to avoid it being interpreted by an outsider as a formal partnership:

1    There ought to be a written agreement, which clearly excludes the concept of partnership and that should be clearly established with Her Majesty's Inspector of Taxes (HMIT) at the outset.
2    Each GDP should have their own nameplate and stationery (letter-headings and appointment cards) otherwise they may be 'holding out' that a partnership exists and consequently stopped from denying it when problems arise.
3    Each party should carefully avoid use of the term 'my partner' in conversation with anyone.
4    It might be sensible to ensure that the annual accounts clearly demonstrate the situation.

Whether the fees are collected at reception from patients and paid into a joint bank account, thereby reducing the individual contributions, is a matter of choice, although it might be appropriate for each GDP's fees, etc. to be kept separate and paid directly into individual practice bank accounts. Earnings by any associate engaged by the 'partnership' should always be collected and paid into the joint bank account.

## Taxation

In the case of a traditional partnership, the tax assessments are raised upon the partnership itself and the individual notices are for information only. The basis of assessment will be the same as for a sole trader (*see* Chapter 15). However, there has been a significant change in the rules for partnerships commencing on or after 19 March 1985. Where there is a change in partnership a new commencement rule will apply. The first four years of the new partnership will be on actual basis, leaving the individuals to elect for either actual or preceding year basis, for the fifth and sixth years. This differs from the sole trader who can choose the basis of assessment for the first three years and thereafter is required to adopt the preceding year basis. The apportionment of the partnership assessment is in accordance with the profit sharing ratio.

# Change of partners

When there is a change in the membership of a partnership (ie either a new partner joins or an existing one retires) the partnership will, for tax purposes, have deemed to have ceased and a new one commenced. However, under Section 113 of the Taxes Act (1988) the partners before and after the date of change may elect for the continuation basis of assessment (which means that they continue to be assessed on the preceding year basis) in which case the change will not constitute a cessation and commencement. Such an election must be signed by all partners, before and after the change, and must be lodged with HMIT within two years of the change. This is a useful tool to reduce tax liabilities, although it should be borne in mind that it will usually be beneficial only where the profits are falling or the number of participating partners is increasing at the point of change.

Example: Black and White were dentists in partnership for many years and were joined on 1 May 1991 by Brown. The taxable profits were agreed as follows:

Year to 30 September:

| | |
|---|---|
| 1986 | £15,000 |
| 1987 | £17,000 |
| 1988 | £16,000 |
| 1989 | £19,000 |
| 1990 | £22,000 |
| 1991 | £24,000 |
| 1992 estimated | £28,000 |
| 1993 estimated | £33,000 |
| 1994 estimated | £40,000 |
| 1995 estimated | £45,000 |
| 1996 estimated | £52,000 |
| 1997 estimated | £50,000 |

The cessation of Black and White is shown as follows:

|  | Normal | Section 63 | Final |
|---|---|---|---|
| 1991/92: actual 6.4.91 to 30.4.92 |  |  | £2000 |
| 1990/91: PYB (ie year to 30.9.89) | £19,000 |  |  |
| or actual 6.4.90 to 5.4.91 (6/12 × £22,000 + |  |  |  |
| 6/12 × £24,000) |  | £23,000 | £23,000 |
| 1989/90 PYB (ie year to 30.9.88) | £16,000 |  |  |
| or actual 6.4.89 to 5.4.90 (6/12 × £22,000 + |  |  |  |
| 6/12 × £19,000) |  | £20,500 | £20,500 |
|  | ———— | ———— | ———— |
|  | £35,000 | £43,500 | £45,500 |

This means that, in the normal course of events, the assessments would have totalled £35,000 but, due to the operation of cessation rules, the assessments will actually be £45,500. The Black, White and Brown commencement is as follows:

|  | Normal | Section 62 | Final |
|---|---|---|---|
| 1991/92: actual 1.5.91 to 5.4.92 |  |  |  |
| (5/12 × £24,000 + 6/12 × £28,000) | £24,000 |  | £24,000 |
| 1992/93: actual 6.4.92 to 5.4.93 |  |  |  |
| (6/12 × £28,000 + 6/12 × £33,000) | £30,500 |  | £30,500 |
| 1993/94: actual 6.4.93 to 5.4.94 |  |  |  |
| (6/12 × £33,000 + 6/12 × £40,000) | £36,500 |  | £36,500 |
| 1994/95: actual 6.4.94 to 5.4.95 |  |  |  |
| (6/12 × £40,000 + 6/12 × £45,000) | £42,500 |  | £42,500 |
| 1995/96: actual 6.4.95 to 5.4.96 |  |  |  |
| (6/12 × £45,000 + 6/12 × £52,000) | £48,500 |  |  |

| or PYB (year to 30.9.94) | | £40,000 | £40,000 |
|---|---|---|---|
| 1996/97: actual 6.4.96 to 5.4.97 | | | |
| (6/12 × £52,000 + 6/12 × £50,000) | £51,000 | | |
| or PYB (year to 30.9.95) | | £45,000 | £45,000 |
| | £99,500 | £85,000 | £218,500 |

The Normal column represents the assessments that would arise if the partners had sought continuation election; the S63 column assumes that the partners do not exercise their right to actual assessment in year 6; the final column is the actual assessments raised. The result if a continuation election was applied would be as follows:

Year of assessments (all on preceding year basis)

| 1989/90 | £16,000 |
|---|---|
| 1990/91 | £19,000 |
| 1991/92 | £22,000 |
| 1992/93 | £24,000 |
| 1993/94 | £28,000 |
| 1994/95 | £33,000 |
| 1995/96 | £40,000 |
| 1996/97 | £45,000 |
| | £227,000 |

The total profits assessed if a continuation election was not made are (£218,500 + £45,500) = £264,000. Therefore, there is a saving of £37,000 (£264,000 − £227,000), ie profits not assessed.

## Conclusion

Generally speaking any GDP would be well advised to give careful consideration to the difficulties before embarking upon a traditional partnership; it would perhaps be more sensible to opt for the 'expense-sharing' association.

# 13

# Understanding accounts

If the book-keeping system in use in the practice is fairly comprehensive, there is no reason why detailed accounts cannot be prepared in a format that will make them a very useful tool for the management of the practice.

## Why prepare accounts?

There is no statutory obligation on a dental surgeon (unless the business is operated by one of the very few dental companies that are subject to special audit regulations) to produce annual accounts. There are, however, several reasons why they should be produced:

1   Most dentists regard the most compelling (and often the only) reason to be as a means of satisfying the Inspector of Taxes as to the taxable profits.
2   In reality accounts may be required to comply with the terms of a partnership (or expense-sharing) agreement, although this is not a statutory duty.
3   To provide evidence to third parties as to the profits being made. For example to answer the needs of the bank or financiers when considering or renewing a loan facility, for mortgage enquiries or for the sale of the practice.
4   Probably quite low down the list, although it should be at the top, is to give the practitioner a means of properly controlling the business.

## Of what do the annual accounts comprise?

A set of accounts for a business comprise three documents and possibly some supporting schedules:

1   The income and expenditure account (sometimes called the profit and loss account). This is a sort of financial history book, which gives a summarized form of the result of the year's trading.

2 The balance sheet, which is effectively a financial snapshot of the business showing its position in terms of money at a particular point in time.

3 The statement of source and application of funds, which explains what has happened to the profit shown in the income and expenditure account. All too often the GDP will question the profit because it is not necessarily reflected in an increased bank balance or funds that can be drawn for the GDP's own use.

# How does a dental practice operate and how is it funded?

Before looking at typical accounts and the sort of information that can be gleaned from them, it would perhaps be appropriate to consider how a dental practice is funded and how it operates in general terms.

## Capital

Like most businesses, the dental practice will have capital that can be divided into:

1 Permanent capital. This is the portion of capital provided by the owner(s) from their own resources. It is supplemented from the excess of profit over personal living expenses (or depleted by any over-drawing for private use). However, it is essential for the existence of the business.

2 Long-term borrowing. This is the loan given to purchase the property, goodwill or equipment at the outset and will be repayable to the bank or financier over a period of (say) ten, fifteen or twenty years, possibly secured by a charge on some security, such as life assurance policy or second charge on a residence.

3 Current liabilities. This is essential short-term borrowing, eg bank overdraft and hire purchase debt. However, it will also include creditors (ie amounts owing to suppliers). Whilst this may not appear to be borrowing, the practice is effectively being run partly on the creditors' capital, a point which is now recognized by some suppliers, who charge interest on overdue accounts.

*Capital gearing*

If the permanent capital is very much less than the total of borrowed capital (long- and short-term) the business is said to be 'high geared' and risky because, in the event of an economic downturn, interest will continue to accrue (often at higher rates) on borrowed money, irrespective of what happens to profit margins. The effects of this were all too apparent during the recession of the late 1980s and early 1990s, as businesses failed due to high interest on substantial borrowing against falling asset values. Had the same businesses been 'low-geared' they would have been far safer as there would have been less interest to pay from diminishing profits. Perhaps the best analogy is a vehicle running down a hill – in low gear there is a greater measure of control and safety.

This may explain why bankers are often very concerned with capital gearing and are inclined, at best, to expect a 1:1 but preferably a 2:1 ratio. Unfortunately, in the past dentists have been such high earners that bankers have been slow to recognize or expect the need for this requirement.

*Relationship between long- and short-term borrowing*

This relationship is also critical. Current liabilities are 'immediately payable' because they do not enjoy the longer contractual delay of the long-term debts. This means that the sensible practitioner will aim to keep the long-term borrowing high in relation to the short-term finance, and certainly the latter should be less than the current assets (see below) otherwise there is a liquidity problem, ie there is a lack of working capital, which would result in embarrassment if all claimants demanded payment simultaneously. The ideal ratio of current assets to short-term liabilities is 2:1.

## Investment of capital

Money raised from these three sources of capital is invested in a dental practice in two ways:

*Fixed assets*

These are those items acquired to run the practice but which are not used up in the course of doing so (although they may wear out, depreciate or amortize over a period). These may be subdivided into:

1   Tangible assets, which can be seen (buildings, equipment and vehicles).
2   Intangible assets, which cannot be seen (goodwill, leases). These are often 'discounted' by lenders as being of doubtful value.

*Current (or circulating) assets*

These effectively earn the profit (Figure 13.1).

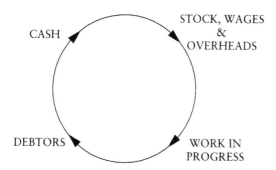

**Figure 13.1**    Current (or circulating) assets which effectively earn the profit

Each time the cycle revolves it will pick up profit and, after deduction of personal drawings, the funds in circulation. However, it would be unwise to assume that the faster the funds circulate the more profitable the business. It is possible for the speed of movement to reach a pitch that will cause the dangerous situation of over-trading, ie operating at a level that is not justified or supported by the capital invested.

The profit earned by the practice is divided between the government (taxes, which effectively drop out of the picture) and the owner, whose share, after deduction of drawings, supplement the capital of the practice.

## Accounting presentation

The operation of the business is presented in accounting terms as shown in Figure 13.2.

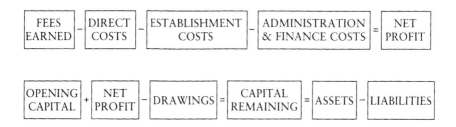

**Figure 13.2**    Operation of the business presented in accounting terms

Of course, these are in what accountants term 'historical cost', which simply means that they represent what happened in money terms relating to the period covered by the accounts. There is no adjustment for inflation and it is likely that to include this would confuse the average dental practitioner, if not the accountant as well.

## Specimen accounts

Several sets of accounts are included in this chapter to illustrate the different formats that are suitable to different circumstances. Each will be explained, after which the chapter will conclude with an 'in-depth' analysis of one of them.

### Mr I. Pullem: sole practitioner

| *I. Pullem: income and expenditure account for the year ended 30 April 1993* | | | |
|---|---|---|---|
| 1992 | | 1993 | 1993 |
| £ | | £ | £ |
| | FEES EARNED | | |
| 61,379 | National Health Service | 82,959 | |
| 8,370 | Private patients | 13,504 | |
| 69,749 | | | 96,463 |
| | DIRECT COSTS | | |
| 5,990 | Materials | 9,780 | |
| 10,716 | Technician charges | 17,945 | |
| 266 | Equipment maintenance | 497 | |
| 7,982 | Nursing salaries | 12,333 | |
| 24,954 | | 40,555 | |
| | ESTABLISHMENT EXPENSES | | |
| 7,020 | Rent | 7,020 | |
| 1,335 | Rates and water (after adjusting rebate) | 1,954 | |
| 1,120 | Heating and lighting | 879 | |
| 681 | Insurance | 701 | |
| | Property maintenance | 214 | |
| 402 | Cleaning and laundry | 186 | |
| 10,558 | | 10,954 | |

| £ | | £ | £ |
|---|---|---|---|
| | MOTOR AND TRAVELLING EXPENSES | | |
| 1,069 | Petrol and oil | 615 | |
| 238 | Repairs and maintenance | 786 | |
| 244 | Licence and insurance | 261 | |
| 42 | Public transport | 107 | |
| 217 | Garage rent | 97 | |
| | Vehicle rental | 175 | |
| 77 | Motoring subscriptions | 85 | |
| 1,887 | | 2,126 | |
| | ADMINISTRATION AND OVERHEAD EXPENSES | | |
| 1,078 | Receptionist's salary | 4,110 | |
| 313 | Postage | 484 | |
| 377 | Printing and stationery | 863 | |
| 836 | Telephone | 882 | |
| 932 | Advertising | 794 | |
| 154 | Staff canteen | 157 | |
| 80 | Protective clothing | 130 | |
| 497 | Courses and conferences | 229 | |
| 161 | Reference books and journals | 104 | |
| 395 | Subscriptions (including MDU) | 761 | |
| 59 | Radiological protection | 66 | |
| 7 | Incidentals | 6 | |
| 4,889 | | 8,586 | |
| | FINANCE COSTS | | |
| 789 | Bank charges | 862 | |
| 13,953 | Bank interest | 12,150 | |
| 423 | Hire purchase charges | 1,662 | |
| 215 | Equipment leasing | 526 | |
| 121 | Credit card service charges | 171 | |
| 15,501 | | 15,371 | |
| 10,037 | Depreciation | 9,405 | |
| 67,826 | | | 86,997 |
| 1,923 | EXCESS OF INCOME OVER EXPENDITURE | | 9,466 |

*I. Pullem: balance sheet as at 30 April 1993*

| 1992 | | 1993 | 1993 |
|---|---|---|---|
| £ | | £ | £ |
| | CAPITAL ACCOUNT | | |
| 26,649 | Balance at 1 May 1992 | | 13,107 |
| 1,923 | Excess of income over expenditure | | 9,466 |
| 28,572 | | | 22,573 |
| 6,104 | Drawings (cash £3740) | 6,924 | |
| 3,188 | Food | 3,347 | |
| 1,140 | Domestic expenses | 1,211 | |
| 2,556 | Life assurance | 2,556 | |
| 640 | Tax | 850 | |
| 215 | National insurance | 215 | |
| 1,622 | Superannuation | 2,234 | |
| 15,465 | | | 17,337 |
| 13,107 | TOTAL NET ASSETS | | 5,236 |
| | LEASE | | |
| 21,592 | Book value at 1 May 1992 | 21,592 | |
| | Amortisation | 5,397 | |
| | | | 16,195 |
| | EQUIPMENT | | |
| 14,726 | Book value at 1 May 1992 | 14,726 | |
| | Additions | 265 | |
| | | 14,991 | |
| | Depreciation | 3,688 | |
| | | | 11,303 |
| | FIXTURES AND FITTINGS | | |
| 674 | Book value at 1 May 1992 | 674 | |
| | Depreciation | 169 | |
| | | | 505 |

| £ | | £ | £ |
|---|---|---|---|
| | MOTOR VEHICLE | | |
| 603 | Book value at 1 May 1992 | 603 | |
| | Depreciation | 151 | |
| | | | 452 |
| 37,595 | | | 28,455 |
| 2,404 | Debtors | 888 | |
| 396 | Stock | 456 | |
| 2,800 | | 1,344 | |
| 3,468 | Hire purchase agreement | 1,583 | |
| 16,458 | Overdraft | 16,163 | |
| 7,362 | Creditors | 6,817 | |
| 27,288 | | 24,563 | |
| 24,488 | Working capital shortfall | | 23,219 |
| 13,107 | TOTAL NET ASSETS | | 5,236 |

---

*I. Pullem: statement of source and application of funds for the year to 30 April 1993*

| | £ |
|---|---|
| SOURCE OF FUNDS | |
| Net profit (adjusted to exclude depreciation) | 18,871 |
| Drawings | 17,337 |
| Retained in practice | 1,534 |
| | |
| APPLICATION OF FUNDS | |
| Additions to equipment | 265 |
| Increase in stock (£456 – £396) | 60 |
| Reduction in overdraft (£16458 – £16163) | 295 |
| Reduction in creditors (£7362 – £6817) | 545 |
| Reduction in hire purchase debt (£3468 – £1583) | 1,885 |
| | 3,050 |
| Reduction in debtors | 1,516 |
| | 1,534 |

## Messrs Crown, Bridge and Brace: expense-sharing 'partnership'

*Messrs Crown, Bridge and Brace income and expenditure account for the year ended 31 December 1992*

|  | 1992 £ | 1992 £ |
|---|---|---|
| Contributions by principals: |  |  |
| Crown | 30,069 |  |
| Bridge | 35,778 |  |
| Brace | 26,950 |  |
|  |  | 92,797 |
| Rental income from flat |  | 2,100 |
|  |  | 94,897 |
| DIRECT COSTS |  |  |
| Materials | 15,048 |  |
| Technician charges | 30,485 |  |
| Nursing and reception salaries | 17,849 |  |
| Equipment maintenance | 1,186 |  |
|  | 64,568 |  |
| ESTABLISHMENT EXPENSES |  |  |
| Rates and water | 1,262 |  |
| Heating and lighting | 1,146 |  |
| Insurance | 584 |  |
| Property maintenance | 3,153 |  |
| Cleaning and laundry | 870 |  |
| Garden | 374 |  |
|  | 7,389 |  |
| ADMINISTRATION AND OVERHEADS |  |  |
| Reception salaries | 13,423 |  |
| Telephone | 590 |  |
| Postage | 2,300 |  |
| Printing and stationery | 580 |  |
| Reference books and journals | 172 |  |

| | £ | £ |
|---|---:|---:|
| Accountancy charges | 518 | |
| Subscriptions | 56 | |
| Advertising | 460 | |
| Debt collection | 19 | |
| Partnership insurance | 36 | |
| Interest on loan | 2,810 | |
| Bank charges | 554 | |
| Christmas festivities | 300 | |
| Protective clothing | 91 | |
| Canteen | 205 | |
| Depreciation | 791 | |
| | 22,905 | |
| Total expenses | | 94,862 |
| OVER-RECOVERY OF EXPENDITURE | | 35 |

*Messrs Crown, Bridge and Brace balance sheet as at 31 December 1992*

| | £ |
|---|---:|
| ACCUMULATED FUNDS | |
| Brought forward | 19,938 |
| Over-recovery of expenditure | 35 |
| TOTAL FUNDS AT 31 DECEMBER 1992 | 19,973 |
| Freehold property | 17,679 |
| Equipment | 2,373 |
| Bank balance | 419 |
| | 20,471 |
| Creditors | 498 |
| TOTAL NET ASSETS | 19,973 |

*Mr Crown income and expenditure account for the year ended 31 December 1992*

|  | 1992 £ | 1992 £ |
|---|---|---|
| Fees earned |  | 57,742 |
| Materials | 145 |  |
| Contribution to joint account | 30,069 |  |
| Laundry and protective clothing | 154 |  |
| Facilities at home as office | 250 |  |
| Telephone | 585 |  |
| Property maintenance | 227 |  |
| Journals and reference books | 17 |  |
| Petrol and oil | 986 |  |
| Motor repairs and maintenance | 3,004 |  |
| Motor licence and insurance | 1,097 |  |
| Motoring subscriptions | 104 |  |
| Other subscriptions | 293 |  |
| Bank charges | 470 |  |
| Cleaning | 28 |  |
| Superannuation | 1,617 |  |
| Repairs and renewals | 46 |  |
| Equipment maintenance | 97 |  |
| Depreciation | 1,442 |  |
|  |  | 40,631 |
| EXCESS OF INCOME OVER EXPENDITURE |  | £17,111 |

*Mr Crown balance sheet as at 31 December 1992*

|  | £ | £ |
|---|---|---|
| CAPITAL ACCOUNT |  |  |
| Balance at 1 January 1992 |  | 14,127 |
| Medical sickness |  | 212 |
| Life assurance |  | 9,563 |
| Facilities at home as office |  | 250 |
| Laundry |  | 154 |
| Dividends |  | 123 |
| Consultancy salary (net) |  | 1,623 |
| Excess of income over expenditure |  | 17,111 |
|  |  | 43,163 |

| | £ | £ |
|---|---|---|
| Drawings | 8,965 | |
| Life assurance | 2,927 | |
| Loan interest | 712 | |
| Holiday | 863 | |
| Income tax and capital gains tax | 9,963 | |
| National insurance | 231 | |
| School fees | 7,999 | |
| Rates and water | 663 | |
| Heat and light | 1,084 | |
| Insurance | 538 | |
| Shares | 1,609 | |
| Mortgage repayments | 2,270 | |
| Pension | 600 | |
| | | 38,424 |
| Deficit at 31 December 1992 | | 4,739 |
| GOODWILL | | 1,000 |
| VEHICLE | | |
| Book value at 1 January 1992 | 3,217 | |
| Additions | 500 | |
| | 3,717 | |
| Depreciation | 929 | |
| | | 2,788 |
| CAR | | |
| Book value at 1 January 1992 | 1,875 | |
| Depreciation | 469 | |
| | | 1,406 |
| EQUIPMENT | | |
| Book value at 1 January 1992 | 176 | |
| Depreciation | 44 | |
| | | 132 |
| | | 5,326 |

|  | £ | £ |
|---|---|---|
| Joint current account | 6,658 | |
| Private (No 2) account | 219 | |
| Abbey National | 15 | |
| | 6,892 | |
| Bank overdraft | 4,479 | |
| Loan account | 3,000 | |
| | 7,479 | |
| Working Capital Shortfall | | 587 |
| TOTAL NET ASSETS | | 4,739 |

*Mr Bridge income and expenditure account for the year ended 31 December 1992*

|  | 1992 £ | 1992 £ |
|---|---|---|
| Fees earned | | 93,189 |
| Contributions to joint account | 35,778 | |
| Cleaning | 108 | |
| Protective clothing | 195 | |
| Laundry | 178 | |
| Facilities at home as office | 300 | |
| Telephone | 305 | |
| Reference books and journals | 47 | |
| Subscriptions | 250 | |
| Bank charges | 12 | |
| Petrol and oil | 1,240 | |
| Motor repairs and maintenance | 2,680 | |
| Motor licence and insurance | 1,043 | |
| Motoring subscriptions | 135 | |
| Superannuation | 3,156 | |
| Depreciation | 3,995 | |
| | | 49,422 |
| EXCESS OF INCOME OVER EXPENDITURE | | 43,767 |

Mr Bridge balance sheet as at 31 December 1993

| | 1992 £ | 1992 £ |
|---|---|---|
| CAPITAL ACCOUNT | | |
| Balance at 1 January 1992 | | 59,915 |
| Dividends | | 522 |
| Bank interest | | 1,400 |
| Wife's salary | | 5,755 |
| Facilities at home | | 300 |
| Laundry allowance | | 178 |
| Sale of boat | | 29,194 |
| Insurance claim | | 2,040 |
| Excess of income over expenditure | | 43,767 |
| | | 143,071 |
| Drawings | 21,554 | |
| Shares | 884 | |
| Life assurance and pensions | 14,528 | |
| National insurance | 231 | |
| Holiday | 8,075 | |
| Domestic rates and water | 973 | |
| Heating and lighting | 765 | |
| Income tax | 21,710 | |
| School fees | 4,747 | |
| Mortgage repayments | 3,392 | |
| | | 76,859 |
| CAPITAL REMAINING AT 31 DECEMBER 1992 | | 66,212 |
| GOODWILL | | 6,000 |
| MOTOR VEHICLES | | |
| Book value at 1 January 1992 | 2,882 | |
| Addition | 13,600 | |
| | 16,482 | |
| Depreciation | 3,496 | |
| | | 12,986 |
| FURNITURE AND EQUIPMENT | | |
| Book value at 1 January 1992 | 1,366 | |
| Addition | 614 | |
| | 1,980 | |

|  | £ | £ |
|---|---|---|
| Depreciation | 495 | |
| | | 1,485 |
| BICYCLE | | |
| Book value at 1 January 1992 | 18 | |
| Depreciation | 5 | |
| | | 13 |
| | | 20,484 |
| Joint current account | 6,658 | |
| Bank balance | 5,333 | |
| Bank balance (personal account) | 1,044 | |
| Cheltenham and Gloucester Building Society | 7,456 | |
| Nationwide Building Society | 14,336 | |
| Special reserve account | 9,061 | |
| Special reserve account | 381 | |
| Cash in transit | 1,620 | |
| | 45,889 | |
| Creditors | 161 | |
| Working capital | | 45,728 |
| TOTAL NET ASSETS | | £66,212 |

---

*Mr Brace income and expenditure account for the year ended 31 December 1992*

| | 1992 £ | 1992 £ |
|---|---|---|
| Fees earned | | 73,303 |
| Contribution to joint account | 26,950 | |
| Rent | 2,100 | |
| Dental materials | 119 | |
| Laundry and protective clothing | 278 | |
| Professional subscriptions | 373 | |
| Equipment maintenance | 74 | |
| Petrol and oil | 1,876 | |
| Motor repairs and maintenance | 361 | |
| Motor licence and insurance | 500 | |
| Motoring subscriptions | 64 | |
| Car parking and incidentals | 5 | |
| Postage and stationery | 39 | |

|  | £ | £ |
|---|---|---|
| Telephone | 487 | |
| Facilities at home | 250 | |
| Professional journals | 51 | |
| Superannuation | 1,848 | |
| Accountancy charges | 200 | |
| Incidentals | 4 | |
| Bank charges and interest | 593 | |
| Loan interest | 4,797 | |
| Insurances | 277 | |
| Depreciation | 2,500 | |
| | | 43,746 |
| EXCESS OF INCOME OVER EXPENDITURE | | £29,557 |

*Mr Brace balance sheet as at 31 December 1992*

| CAPITAL ACCOUNT | £ | £ |
|---|---|---|
| Balance at 1 January 1992 | | 16,646 |
| Deposit account interest | | 53 |
| Facilities at home | | 250 |
| Excess of income over expenditure | | 29,557 |
| | | 46,506 |
| Drawings | 35,794 | |
| Community charge | 325 | |
| National insurance | 232 | |
| Life assurance | 2,237 | |
| Income tax | 5,077 | |
| Holiday | 1,006 | |
| | | 44,671 |
| CAPITAL REMAINING AT 31 DECEMBER 1992 | | 1,835 |
| Goodwill | | 22,000 |

|  | £ | £ |
|---|---:|---:|
| MOTOR VEHICLE |  |  |
| Book value at 1 January 1992 | 10,000 |  |
| Depreciation | 2,500 |  |

|  | £ | £ |
|---|---:|---:|
|  | 7,500 |  |
|  |  | 29,500 |
| Joint current account | 6,658 |  |
| Bank account | 3,348 |  |
| Special reserve account | 633 |  |
|  | 10,639 |  |
| Bank account (no. 2) | 4,855 |  |
| Car loan | 3,213 |  |
| Practice account | 30,036 |  |
| Creditors | 200 |  |
|  | 38,304 |  |
| Working capital shortfall |  | 27,665 |
| TOTAL NET ASSETS |  | 1,835 |

---

Messrs Black and White: expense-sharing 'partnership'

*Income and expenditure account for the year ended 30 April 1992*

|  | 1992 £ | 1992 £ |
|---|---:|---:|
| Fees earned |  | 91,525 |
| DIRECT COSTS |  |  |
| Materials | 23,104 |  |
| Associate's remuneration | 7,397 |  |
| Technician charges | 7,478 |  |
| Staff salaries | 53,214 |  |
| Equipment maintenance | 2,251 |  |
| Replacement of instruments | 291 |  |
|  | 93,735 |  |

|  | £ | £ |
|---|---:|---:|
| ESTABLISHMENT EXPENSES | | |
| Rates and water | 2,387 | |
| Heating and lighting | 1,672 | |
| Insurance | 906 | |
| Property maintenance | 371 | |
| Gardening | 523 | |
| Laundry and cleaning | 931 | |
| | 6,790 | |

| | £ | £ |
|---|---:|---:|
| ADMINISTRATION AND OVERHEADS | | |
| Telephone | 1,688 | |
| Postage | 1,396 | |
| Computer supplies | 36 | |
| Printing and stationery | 1,670 | |
| Bank charges | 739 | |
| Bank interest (including loan) | 2,326 | |
| Accountancy charges | 500 | |
| Radiological protection | 235 | |
| Staff canteen | 1,104 | |
| Christmas festivities | 510 | |
| Staff gratuities/gifts | 65 | |
| First aid | 2 | |
| Incidentals | 30 | |
| Donations | 12 | |
| Aquarium expenses | 222 | |
| Protective clothing | 138 | |
| Repairs and renewals | 450 | |
| Licence | 25 | |
| Flowers | 62 | |
| Reference books and journals | 143 | |
| Equipment leasing | 2,228 | |
| Debt collecting | 44 | |
| Staff training | 174 | |
| Staff travelling | 35 | |
| Sundries | 6,886 | |
| Business meals | 134 | |
| | 20,854 | |

|  | £ | £ |
|---|---:|---:|
| FINANCE COSTS | | |
| Mortgage interest | 9,545 | |
| Partnership insurance | 4,001 | |
| | 13,546 | |
| Depreciation | 4,320 | |
| | | 139,245 |
| TOTAL NET EXPENDITURE | | 47,720 |
| Divisible as to: | | |
| Mr Black | | 27,277 |
| Mr White | | 20,443 |
| | | 47,720 |

---

*Messrs Black and White balance sheet as at 30 April 1992*

|  | 1992 £ | 1992 £ |
|---|---:|---:|
| CAPITAL ACCOUNT | | |
| Mr Black | | |
| Balance at 1 May 1991 | 45,316 | |
| Share of net expenditure | 27,277 | |
| | 72,593 | |
| Contributed during the year | 44,000 | |
| | | 28,593 |
| Mr White | | |
| Balance at 1 May 1991 | 17,562 | |
| Share of net expenditure | 20,443 | |
| | 38,005 | |
| Contributed during the year | 21,750 | |
| | | 16,255 |
| DEFICIT AT 30 APRIL 1992 | | 44,848 |

|  | £ | £ |
|---|---|---|
| GOODWILL | | 10,000 |
| FREEHOLD PROPERTY | | 63,163 |
| EQUIPMENT AND FURNISHINGS | | |
| Book value at 1 May 1991 | 16,569 | |
| Additions | 709 | |
| | 17,278 | |
| Depreciation | 4,320 | |
| | | 12,958 |
| | | 86,121 |
| Bank account | 2,269 | |
| Cash float | 124 | |
| | 2,393 | |
| Mortgage | 125,000 | |
| Loan | 7,669 | |
| Creditors | 536 | |
| Credit cards | 157 | |
| | 133,362 | |
| Working capital shortfall | | 130,969 |
| DEFICIT AT 30 APRIL 1992 | | 44,848 |

---

Messrs Brown and Green: traditional partnership

*Joint expenditure account for the year ended 15 August 1993*

|  | 1993 £ | 1993 £ |
|---|---|---|
| Fees earned | | 166,022 |
| DIRECT COSTS | | |
| Dental materials | 12,923 | |
| Wages (including technician charges) | 21,912 | |
| Equipment maintenance and replacement of instruments | 55 | |
| | 34,890 | |

|                                   | £       | £       |
|-----------------------------------|--------:|--------:|
| ESTABLISHMENT EXPENSES            |         |         |
| Rent                              | 2,645   |         |
| Rates and water                   | 1,458   |         |
| Service charge                    | 230     |         |
| Heating and lighting              | 1,865   |         |
| Insurance                         | 239     |         |
| Cleaning                          | 168     |         |
| Property maintenance              | 1,049   |         |
|                                   | 7,654   |         |
|                                   |         |         |
| ADMINISTRATION AND OVERHEADS      |         |         |
| Telephone                         | 818     |         |
| Postage                           | 428     |         |
| Printing and stationery           | 792     |         |
| Advertising                       | 180     |         |
| Bank charges                      | 1,221   |         |
| Subscriptions                     | 305     |         |
| Protective clothing               | 429     |         |
| Staff canteen                     | 335     |         |
| Partnership fees                  | 609     |         |
| Accountancy charges               | 150     |         |
| Courses                           | 12      |         |
| Toys for waiting room             | 60      |         |
| Legal costs                       | 267     |         |
| Repairs and renewals – towels     | 24      |         |
| Bad debts                         | 105     |         |
|                                   | 5,735   |         |
|                                   |         |         |
| Depreciation                      | 4,913   |         |
|                                   |         | 53,192  |
|                                   |         |         |
| NET PROFIT                        |         | 112,830 |
|                                   |         |         |
| Divisible as to:                  |         |         |
| Mr Brown 60%                      |         | 67,698  |
| Mr Green 40%                      |         | 45,132  |
|                                   |         | 112,830 |

*Joint balance sheet as at 15 August 1993*

|  | 1993 £ | 1993 £ |
|---|---|---|
| CAPITAL ACCOUNT |  |  |
| Mr Brown |  |  |
| Introduced | 5,000 |  |
| Excess of income over expenditure | 67,698 |  |
|  | 72,698 |  |
| Drawings | 30,939 |  |
|  |  | 41,759 |
| Mr Green |  |  |
| Introduced | 3,000 |  |
| Excess of income over expenditure | 45,132 |  |
|  | 48,132 |  |
| Drawings | 23,214 |  |
|  |  | 24,918 |
|  |  | 66,677 |
| GOODWILL |  | 24,000 |
| FREEHOLD AND LEASEHOLD PROPERTIES |  | 36,000 |
| EQUIPMENT AND FURNISHINGS |  |  |
| At cost | 12,000 |  |
| Additions | 7,650 |  |
|  | 19,650 |  |
| Depreciation | 4,913 |  |
|  |  | 14,737 |
|  |  | 74,737 |
| Overdraft | 3,785 |  |
| Loan | 4,124 |  |
| Creditors | 451 |  |
|  |  | 8,360 |
| TOTAL NET ASSETS |  | 66,377 |

For the sake of simplicity, comparative figures (ie those for the previous year printed on the left-hand side) and the statement of source and application of funds have been omitted from all but the first and last accounts. Under normal circumstances they would form part of the accounts as a matter of routine:

## Accounts of a sole practitioner

The format is fairly straightforward but it will been seen that the income and expenditure account has been divided into 'blocks' of expense. The direct costs are the most important because they represent items directly associated with output.

## Expense-sharing associations

### Expense-sharing association with three principals but no associate

A 'pool' account sets out the joint expenditure and the contribution made by each principal from their individual accounts. The contributions will differ according to:

1  Gross fee income.
2  Technician charges.

The actual apportionment will depend wholly upon the agreement between the parties. It will also be seen that at the end there is a small over- or under-recovery of expenditure, which is carried forward to an accumulated fund in the balance sheet. The amount in this fund is represented by the joint assets less joint liabilities (held equally). From the individual practitioner's accounts it will be seen that the contributions received into the joint account are included in the individual accounts as an expense. The share in the joint account is also shown as an asset on the balance sheet. All four accounts clearly link together, although the individual practitioners see only their own figures.

### Expense-sharing association of two principals and an associate

Here it will be seen that the associate's earnings and expenses are included in the 'pool' account, thereby reducing the contribution to be made by each individual principal. However, in this case the principals meet their own technicians' charges and professional subscriptions. Again, the variation is due in this case to the difference in gross fee income between the principals, whose individual accounts are now reproduced.

In both the expense-sharing cases the joint expenditure (and, where appropriate, income) is dealt with through a 'pool', and the individual fee income and expenses (including the contribution into the pool) are shown in the principals' own accounts. This differs from the treatment adopted by some accountants, who split the joint expenditure and include it as itemized expenditure in the individual accounts. That is not a practice to be encouraged because it will make any form of statistical analysis or comparison exceedingly difficult, consequently detracting from the value of the accounts other than for tax purposes.

## Traditional partnership accounts

These are effectively identical to those of a sole practitioner except that the final profit is divided according to the partnership agreement (or equally, if none exists).

## Allocation of expenditure

The allocation of expenditure within the accounts is very much a matter of individual choice, although the rules relating to deduction of expenses for tax purposes are fairly clear-cut. Generally, the major items are:

1   Dental materials, which will usually include disposables such as bibs, paper towels, paper cups, and mouthwash tablets.
2   Technician charges (laboratory fees).
3   Hygienist's remuneration.
4   Associate's remuneration.
5   Anaesthetist's fees, where general anaesthetic is administered.
6   DSA salaries (but not reception salaries or, where there is overlap, a sum representing reception work is usually transferred to administration costs).
7   Equipment maintenance, to include replacement of hand instruments (which will necessitate transfer from the dental suppliers' accounts which may have been analysed to materials).
8   Laundry and cleaning of the surgeries themselves.
9   Establishment expenses, which relate to the provision of the premises, including the services such as heat and light, insurance, property maintenance, water rates, etc.
10  Administration expenses, which will usually cover all the office and associated costs.
11  Finance costs, which will be those items such as bank interest, credit card service charges, debt collecting and hire purchase interest that arise from funding the practice.

12    Drawings. It will be seen that in most instances the personal expenditure is analysed in broad terms. This is done to minimize the enquiries from HMIT and also to give the GDP a fairly general idea of how the money is being spent. It is perhaps surprising that few dentists really know how their money is being used.

## Accounting ratios

A number of ratios are of interest and it is important to bear in mind that the Inspector of Taxes will be aware not only of these but also of the national averages. It is always wise to remember that the inspector will be looking at the accounts critically and that problems can often be avoided by drawing their attention to any anomalies and offering an explanation before questions are asked. Experience has shown that many Inland Revenue staff are rather too quick to rush into an investigation simply because they do not appreciate the significance of variations in some of the income/expenditure patterns.

## Accounts analysis

The accounts below are a full set of typical accounts for a mixed NHS/ private practice in a rural area close to a small town that lacks NHS facilities.

| *Mr Drillemall income and expenditure account for the year ended 31 December 1993* | | |
|---|---|---|
| | 1993 £ | 1993 £ |
| FEES EARNED | | |
| National Health Service | | 186,162 |
| Private patients | | 11,312 |
| Denplan | | 8,511 |
| | | 205,985 |
| DIRECT COSTS | | |
| Materials | 20,723 | |
| Technician charges | 42,351 | |
| Equipment maintenance and replacement of instruments | 1,987 | |

|  | £ | £ |
|---|---:|---:|
| Locum | 8,475 | |
| Hygienist | 2,511 | |
| Nursing and reception salaries | 24,391 | |
| | 100,438 | |

ESTABLISHMENT EXPENSES

| | | |
|---|---:|---:|
| Rates and water | 1,614 | |
| Heating and lighting | 1,670 | |
| Insurance | 919 | |
| Laundry and cleaning | 906 | |
| Gardening | 316 | |
| Property maintenance | 3,323 | |
| | 8,748 | |

ADMINISTRATION AND OVERHEADS

| | | |
|---|---:|---:|
| Receptionist's salary | 11,200 | |
| Telephone | 637 | |
| Printing and stationery | 1,868 | |
| Postage | 937 | |
| Bank charges | 737 | |
| Bank interest | 117 | |
| Advertising | 376 | |
| Accountancy charges | 655 | |
| Subscriptions | 513 | |
| Repairs and renewals | 66 | |
| Donations | 93 | |
| Petrol and oil | 1,380 | |
| Motor repairs and maintenance | 1,127 | |
| Motor licence and insurance | 803 | |
| Pager rental | 157 | |
| Staff canteen | 651 | |
| Taxis and rail fares | 108 | |
| Reference books and journals | 248 | |
| Flowers | 21 | |
| Debt collecting | 41 | |
| Signwriting | 38 | |
| Protective clothing | 426 | |
| Equipment leasing | 6,332 | |
| Hire purchase charges | 1,813 | |
| Denplan literature | 209 | |
| Christmas festivities | 85 | |

|  | £ | £ |
|---|---|---|
| Sundries | 42 | |
| Profit on sale of vehicle | − 887 | |
| Depreciation | 3,941 | |
| | 33,734 | |
| Total expenditure | | 142,920 |
| EXCESS OF INCOME OVER EXPENDITURE | | 63,065 |

---

*Mr Drillemall balance sheet as at 31 December 1993*

|  | 1992 £ | 1992 £ |
|---|---|---|
| CAPITAL ACCOUNT | | |
| Balance at I January 1993 | | 22,362 |
| Wife's salary as lecturer | | 11,127 |
| Interest received | | 224 |
| Excess of income over expenditure | | 63,065 |
| | | 96,778 |
| Drawings (including £6500 cash) | 13,813 | |
| Building work at home | 3,749 | |
| Food paid for by cheque etc. | 1,320 | |
| Rates and water | 940 | |
| Heating and lighting | 1,637 | |
| Insurance | 1,224 | |
| Life assurance premiums and pensions | 6,793 | |
| Private medical insurance | 1,009 | |
| National insurance | 369 | |
| Mortgage repayments | 9067 | |
| Income tax | 6144 | |
| Superannuation | 4310 | |
| | | 50,375 |
| CAPITAL REMAINING AT 31 DECEMBER 1993 | | 46,403 |
| Freehold property | | 8264 |

|  | £ | £ |
|---|---:|---:|
| EQUIPMENT |  |  |
| Book value at 1 January 1993 | 3,687 |  |
| Additions | 362 |  |
|  | 4,049 |  |
| Depreciation | 1,012 |  |
|  |  | 3037 |
| COMPUTER |  |  |
| At cost | 2,413 |  |
| Depreciation | 603 |  |
|  |  | 1810 |
| FURNITURE |  |  |
| Book value at 1 January 1993 | 706 |  |
| Depreciation | 176 |  |
|  |  | 530 |
| MOTOR VEHICLE |  |  |
| Book value at 1 January 1993 | 7,419 |  |
| Part-exchanged | 8,306 |  |
| Profit on sale | 887 |  |
| Addition – at cost | 21,978 |  |
| Depreciation | 2,000 |  |
|  |  | 19,978 |
| MOTOR VEHICLE |  |  |
| Book value at 1 January 1993 | 600 |  |
| Depreciation | 150 |  |
|  |  | 450 |
|  |  | 34,069 |
| Building society | 15,821 |  |
| Bank balance – Trustee Savings Bank | 2,933 |  |
| Debtors – NHI | 8,977 |  |
| Debtors – private | 5,095 |  |
| Stock | 1482 |  |
| Cash float | 62 |  |
|  | 34,370 |  |

|  | £ | £ |
|---|---|---|
| Hire purchase agreements | 17,090 | |
| Creditors | 4,946 | |
| | 22,036 | |
| Working capital | | 12,334 |
| TOTAL NET ASSETS | | 46,403 |

---

*Mr Drillemall statement of source and application of funds for the year ended 31 December 1993*

|  | £ | £ |
|---|---|---|
| NET PROFIT | | 63,065 |
| Adjust for transactions not involving the movement of money (ie paper entries): | | |
| – depreciation | 3,941 | |
| – profit on car | 887 | |
| | | 3,054 |
| | | 66,119 |
| ADDITIONAL ASSETS | | |
| Equipment | 362 | |
| Computer | 2,413 | |
| Car | 21,978 | |
| | 24,753 | |
| Sale proceeds of old car | 8,306 | |
| | | 16,447 |
| Deposited in building society | | 15,821 |
| Increase in debtors and stock (£15,554-£8552) | | 7.002 |
| Increase in cash float | | 62 |
| | | 39,332 |
| Funded by: | | |
| – reduction in bank (£5140–£2933) | 2,207 | |
| – increase in hire purchase (£17,090–£9165) | 7,925 | |
| – increase in creditors (£4946–£2841) | 2,105 | |

|  | £ 12,237 | £ |
|---|---|---|
|  |  | 27,095 |
| Drawings | 50,375 |  |
| Introduced: |  |  |
| – salary | 11,127 |  |
| – interest | £24 |  |
|  |  | 39,024 |
|  |  | 66,119 |

By expressing the figures in percentage terms and comparing them with the national averages for a 'one-man' practice in a similar environment, it is possible to identify if there are areas of wastage or other problems:

|  | Actual | National |
|---|---|---|
| Fee income: |  |  |
| – NHS | 90.38 | 85.56 |
| – private | 5.49 | 11.46 |
| – Denplan | 4.13 | 3.02 |
|  | 100.00 |  |
| Materials | 10.06 | 8.21 |
| Technician | 20.56 | 21.46 |
| Equipment maintenance | 0.96 | 0.82 |
| Locum | 4.11 | 3.32 |
| Hygienist | 1.22 | 2.90 |
| Nursing salaries | 11.84 | 14.44 |
|  | 48.75 |  |
| Establishment costs | 4.75 | 5.82 |
| (if a notional economic rent is included this would be 9.93%) |  |  |
| Administration | 16.38 | 18.22 |
| Stationery | 0.09 |  |
| Motoring | 1.61 |  |
| Leasing/hire purchase | 3.94 |  |
| NET PROFIT | 26.77 | 24.04 |

Apart from the question of profitability and comparison of expense, there are the questions of stock-holding and leverage to be considered.

## Stock-holding

The average stock of materials in the specimen accounts was £1415 (1398 + 1482 ÷ 2). By dividing this into the amount of stock used (£20,723), we obtain the annual stock-turnover rate: 14.64, which means there is on average 3 weeks stock (52 divided by 14.64). This is probably a satisfactory level, considering the stocks carried by suppliers and the short 'lead time' (delivery period after orders are placed).

The private fee book debts averaged £4790 (4485 + 5095 ÷ 2). The private fee income was £11,312 which means that the leverage (the debtor turnover rate) is 2.36 per annum (£11,312 divided by 4790) or 22 weeks (52 ÷ 2.36), which is far too high. This is a low geared practice: owner's capital averages (£46,403 + £22,362 ÷ 2) = £34,382; borrowed capital is £22,036 = 1.5:1. Liquidity is also good (£34,370:£22,036) = 1.5:1. These are generally the sort of facts that can be extracted quickly from accounts provided the original records are accurate and the data readily accessible.

## Greater detail

The following illustration is much more complex (it reproduces a portion of the accounts) and does, of course, necessitate very carefully maintained records. As the records were very detailed, it is possible to analyse the accounts so as to show the profitability of individual practitioners within the surgery. The income of the individual practitioners has been ascertained from the counter-book (as described in Chapter 9). The hygienist's earnings are identified from the day-book, which is maintained by the hygienist in the surgery and shows the work done on behalf of each individual practitioner. The materials used by the practitioners in their surgeries has been ascertained by maintenance of the stock issue forms (Chapter 6).

*Mr D. Kay analysed income and expenditure account*

| | Principal | Associate 1 | Associate 2 | Associate 3 | Hygienist | Total |
|---|---|---|---|---|---|---|
| Fees earned: | | | | | | |
| – NHS | £8467 | £107,627 | £92,888 | £83,012 | | £291,994 |
| – private | £139,778 | £1634 | £2253 | | | £143,665 |
| | £148,245 | £109,261 | £95,141 | £83,012 | | £435,659 |
| Hygienist's Fees (included in principal's and associates' accounts) | £16,307 | £3278 | £3222 | | £22,807 | |
| Net dental earnings | £131,938 | £105,983 | £91,919 | £83,012 | £22,807 | £435,659 |
| Materials | £8555 | £6539 | £4320 | £1183 | £1398 | £21,995 |
| Technician – actual | £18,206 | £10,002 | £7819 | £8329 | | £44,356 |
| Associates' remuneration | | £49,357 | £42,807 | £38,068 | | £130,232 |
| Hygienist's remuneration | | | | | £9503 | £9503 |
| Nurse | £8526 | £6506 | £6791 | £7004 | | £28,827 |
| Balance | £96,651 | £33,579 | £30,182 | £28,428 | £11,906 | £200,746 |
| Establishment | £4285 | £4285 | £4285 | £4285 | £2143 | £19,283 |
| Administration | £19,023 | £6609 | £5941 | £5597 | £2343 | £39,513 |
| NET PROFIT | £73,343 | £22,685 | £19,956 | £18,546 | £7420 | £141,950 |

# 14

# Personal taxation

Whilst there has always been some form of taxation in the UK, some of it today appears rather amusing (window tax, wig tax, bachelor tax). Income tax in its present form was introduced by William Pitt who needed to raise funds for the Napoleonic Wars; afterwards the tax was abolished, although it was later reintroduced. Gladstone was committed to its abolition and, indeed, he did get the rate down to 3d (roughly 1p in modern money) in the £, but he never succeeded in its complete withdrawal.

The highest rates of tax were seen in the early 1950s when income tax reached 10s6d (52.5p) in the £ plus surtax on incomes over £2000 per annum ranging to a further 9s0d (45p) in the £. Although today we complain at the high rate of direct taxation, it is considerably lower than in the decade following World War II.

Today, income tax stands at 20p in the £ on the first £2500 of income (known as the lower rate), and at 25p in the £ for amounts between £2501 and £23,700. Taxable income in excess of £23,701 per annum is chargeable at 40p in the £. Contrary to popular belief, there is no longer any distinction between earned and unearned income for the purpose of computing tax liability – all income is charged at the same rate, the distinction having disappeared some years ago. Income Tax is technically a temporary tax and if Parliament were to fail to pass the Finance Act its collection would be unlawful; this has not yet happened.

## Structure of the Inland Revenue

The ultimate jurisdiction over the tax system lies with the Board of Inland Revenue, but various branches deal with the day-to-day operations.

### Inspector of taxes

This is the department with which most taxpayers have their first encounter. Most large towns will have one or more tax offices which deal with the affairs of working taxpayers or with their place of business in that district. The tax office is under the control of a District Inspector, who has a number of individual inspectors and clerical officers/assistants. Broadly their duties are:

1  To issue the annual income tax returns.
2  To examine the completed returns and accounts submitted by or on behalf of the self-employed.
3  The preparation and issue of assessment notices (Schedule D for the self-employed and Schedule E for employees) including those for other income such as rents.
4. Dealing with appeals against estimated assessments.
5  Correspondence with taxpayers and their advisers.
6  Listing appeals and conducting the case on behalf of the Inland Revenue.
7  Issue of notices of coding for employed persons and  generally overseeing the operation of PAYE.
8  Conducting 'in-depth' investigations on accounts where it is felt that there may be something amiss.

## Collector of taxes

This is a separate section, although in recent years there have been proposals to integrate the Inspectors and Collectors of Taxes to save expense and reduce problems.

There are two central accounts offices – one at Cumbernauld and the other at Shipley – which are computerized and issue:

1  Assessments on instructions from the Inspector of Taxes.
2  Notices for postponement of tax.
3  Demands for payment.

These offices collect the greater proportion of taxes but where there are collection difficulties the matter is ultimately passed to the local Collector of Taxes, who will make a direct application before exercising distraint on property or issuing legal proceedings through the Courts.

Regrettably, the Inland Revenue has been under enormous pressure in recent years and the government's need for funds and the low calibre of staff working for the Inland Revenue have caused many problems for taxpayers.

# Enforcement office

In extreme cases it is sometimes necessary to consider bankruptcy proceedings in order to recover tax, and these cases are referred initially to the Enforcement Office and thereafter to the Inland Revenue Solicitor in London, who will present the petition to the High Court.

# Enquiry and Special Branch

These departments are concerned with serious investigations where the amount of tax lost is expected to be comparatively high or where the case is regarded as of a serious nature. Fortunately few dental surgeons find themselves entangled with these offices, but those who do so need to ensure they are professionally represented from the outset.

# Technical division

This is concerned primarily with advising the Inland Revenue on technical points and is effectively an internal department.

# Superannuation funds office

The approval of superannuation schemes and matters involved with pension funds fall within the jurisdiction of this office.

# General and special commissioners

Disputes between the taxpayer and the Inspector of Taxes are usually resolved by an independent body of businessmen (somewhat akin to magistrates) who meet at regular intervals to hear appeals or contentious issues. They are assisted by a full-time clerk and their decisions are, save on a point of law, final and binding. Hearings are informal and held in private; the decisions are not reported.

The Special Commissioners are full-time officials with specialist knowledge; they have the same duties as the General Commissioners but usually meet at a central point (Thames Ditton) to hear cases on an *ad hoc* basis. Their decisions are not reported but are available to the Inspector of Taxes.

# Appeals

Appeals against the decision of either the General or Special Commissioners against points of law are heard by the Court of Appeal, with any subsequent appeal going to the House of Lords. The majority of cases are finally settled at local level because the cost of an appeal would be horrendous and often not worthwhile particularly bearing in mind that the loser will usually have to pay both their own costs and the costs of their opponent. Costs are not awarded by the General or Special Commissioners.

# Tax schedules

Income is classified for the purpose of assessment into various tax schedules, each with their own rules of assessment and dates for payment. A more detailed explanation is given in Chapter 15.

# Allowances

Every taxpayer is entitled to certain allowances against income, irrespective of its source or nature. This is quite distinct from the expenses that are allowable against income.

# Personal allowance

Every taxpayer is entitled to the basic personal allowance of £3445 up to the age of 65. Over that age there is age relief, which is dealt with below.

## Married couple's allowance

A married man is entitled to married couple's allowance of £1720 for a full year or £143.33 for each month he was married in any tax year. There are provisions for this allowance to be assigned to the wife but it is only viable when she is the higher earner.

## Age relief

The allowances are £4200 between the ages of 65 and 75 and £4370 over that age. The married couple's allowance also applies where the elder spouse is between 65 and 75, with an increase of £40 over that age. Age allowance is abated by £1 for each £2 of income exceeding £14,200.

## Widow's bereavement allowance

A special allowance of £1720 is given to a widow for the year in which her spouse dies and for the following year of assessment. However if she remarries before the start of the second year the following year's relief is withdrawn.

## Child relief

Child relief was abolished some years ago and parents are now paid Child Benefit, £9.65 per week for the eldest child and £7.80 per week for other children. However, a single parent family does qualify for an allowance of £1720 for a child.

## Blind person's allowance

A special allowance of £1,080 is given to each blind person.

## Life assurance relief

This is now available only for contracts made before 14 March 1984. It is given by deduction at 12.5% on the premium paid to the insurance company.

## Expenses

Certain trades and profession have an agreed standard deduction to cover expenses of employed persons. There is no such allowance for a dental surgeon, although an employed dentist is entitled to deductions for professional subscriptions (GDC registration fee, subscription to MPS, MDU, BDA and other approved professional bodies) provided these are not paid by the employer. The dental surgeon may also be entitled to other expenses, but this will depend entirely on individual circumstances.

## Pension funds

NHS Superannuation is allowable for tax purposes but dental practitioners may, if they wish, forgo this allowance in favour of a private pension scheme, which is otherwise only allowable on private fee income. The allowance is:

| Age at the beginning of the year of assessment | Maximum (%) |
|---|---|
| Under 35 | 17 |
| 36 to 45 | 20 |
| 46 to 50 | 25 |
| 51 to 55 | 30 |
| 56 to 60 | 35 |
| 61 or over | 40 |

There is a cap on earnings that can be used for pension contributions:

| | |
|---|---|
| 1989/90 | 60000 |
| 1990/91 | 64800 |
| 1991/92 | 71400 |
| 1992/93 | 75000 |

## Retirement annuities

There is an allowance for retirement annuities as follows:

| Age at start of year | Maximum (%) |
| --- | --- |
| Under 50 | 17 |
| 51 to 55 | 20 |
| 56 to 60 | 22.5 |
| Over 61 | 40 |

There are certain restrictions on partnership retirement annuities and on the life assurance element of both private pensions and retirement annuities; but these are too complicated to consider here.

## Maintenance payments

Maintenance payments are given only for Court Orders made before 15 March 1988. The amount is restricted to £1720.

## National Savings Bank interest

The first £70 of interest is exempt (this applies to both husband and wife independently).

## Medical premiums

From 6 April 1990 premiums under an eligible contract for private medical insurance have been given to UK residents over 60 years of age. Basic rate is given by deduction at source but higher rate relief has to be claimed.

# Independent taxation

In April 1990 the Independent Taxation system was introduced, under which a husband and wife are automatically assessed separately (prior to that date an election had to be made). This means that each spouse is responsible for his or her own tax and entitled to the appropriate personal allowances. Bearing in mind that it is often the case that a GDP husband has a larger income than his wife, it could be beneficial for all investments to be in the wife's name, so that income on them are taxed at standard rate in the wife's name rather than at higher rates in the husband's name (or vice versa).

# Employment

·Where a GDP has, in addition to dental practice profits, a salary from a hospital or educational appointment (or a pension) it may well be that the tax can become complicated due to involvement of more than one tax office. The personal allowance will usually be given against the salary/pension taxed under Schedule E, leaving the practice profits to be taxed without personal allowances under Schedule D.

# Mortgage interest relief

Relief is given for interest on the first £30,000 of a mortgage on the GDP's dwelling house. Usually this is by way of MIRAS, which means that the bank or building society is paid at a lower rate to reflect the tax relief. However, where for some reason it is not given in that way, it is by way of adjustment in the tax assessment.

Interest on mortgages raised for purchase of business premises or for loans in connection with the business are allowable for tax purposes and will normally be given by way of a deduction against the practice profits before arriving at the taxable profit. However, where the capital account is overdrawn, HMIT may well argue that the finance was raised effectively to make good the excess of drawings over profits and consequently it was not for the purpose of the business. In such a case the interest is not allowable. As depreciation is not a cash outlay it may be necessary to add back depreciation to the capital account to determine whether or to what extent it was overdrawn. Care ought to be taken to ensure that only that part of the borrowing that relates to overdrawn capital is disallowed.

Where the practice is clearly solvent it may well be feasible to create a situation where the business repays part of the capital to the owner, who can use the funds however they wish. Any funds raised subsequently to replace the drawn capital will be a business loan and the interest will be allowable. It is essential that the sequence of events is clearly established and documented if such an arrangement is to succeed.

## Covenants

Where the GDP pays standard rate tax, any covenanted payment made to a charitable organisation can be accompanied by a tax deduction certificate, which would enable the charity to recover the tax from the Inland Revenue. Effectively, the GDP is donating their own money and also an equivalent amount of tax.

## Example of an assessment

A GDP has practice profits of £52,000, less capital allowances of £4000, and with a salary of £7000 from a hospital appointment (received net of £1750 tax).   Rental income was £3000 after deduction of expenses and there was building society interest of £1800. The dentist is married with a mortgage of £30,000 at 9% not subject to MIRAS. Pension contributions are 6% of the salary and there is a private pension policy on which the premium is £8400. Dividends totalled £3000   (tax credits £1000).

| EARNED INCOME | £ | £ | Tax Credit (£) |
|---|---|---|---|
| Schedule D.11  profits from Dentistry | | 52,000 | |
| Less: | | | |
| – capital allowances | | 4,000 | |
| | | 48,000 | |
| Schedule E Hospital Employment (Gross) | | 8,750 | 1,750 |
| | | £56,750 | |
| INVESTMENT INCOME | | | |
| Schedule A rent received | 3,000 | | |
| Schedule F dividends (gross) | 4,000 | | 1,000 |
| Schedule  D III bank interest (gross) | 2,400 | | 600 |
| | 9,400 | | |
| | £66,150 | | |

|                                | £      | £         | £     |
|--------------------------------|--------|-----------|-------|
| ALLOWANCES                     |        |           |       |
| Mortgage interest              | 2,700  |           |       |
| Class 4 N/C relief             | 472    |           |       |
| Personal                       | 3,445  |           |       |
| Married                        | 1,720  |           |       |
| Personal pension               | 8,400  |           |       |
| Employment pension             | 525    | 17,262    |       |
|                                |        |           |       |
| Taxable income                 |        | 48,888    |       |
|                                |        |           |       |
|                                |        |           | 3,350 |
| INCOME TAX & N/C               |        |           |       |
| £2,500 @ 20%                   |        | 500.00    |       |
| £21,200 @ 25%                  |        | 5,300.00  |       |
| £25,188 @ 40%                  |        | 10,075.20 |       |
|                                |        |           |       |
|                                |        | 15,875.20 |       |
| Mortgage interest £2,700 @ 15% |        | 405.00    |       |
| (restricted to basic rate allowance) |        |           |       |
|                                |        | 16,280.20 |       |
| Less tax credits               |        | 3,350.00  |       |
|                                |        |           |       |
|                                |        | 12,930.20 |       |
| Class 4 N/C                    |        | 941.22    |       |
|                                |        |           |       |
|                                |        | 13,871.42 |       |

The above calculation is the total taxable income under the various Schedules. However, as explained in Chapter 15, the assessments will be raised separately under the different schedules. As the GDP is a higher rate tax payer, the employment income and investment incomes must be grossed (including the tax credits) to be taxed at 40%.

# 15

# Business taxation

Whilst it is perhaps the fairest system in the world, UK tax is perhaps also one of the most complicated. Income tax is a direct method of taxation but it can be raised either by direct assessment or by deduction at source. All income is taxed according to its source and each is classified by reference to Schedules set out in tax law each with its own assessment rules.

| Type of Income | Schedules |
|---|---|
| Income from property in the UK (eg rent from unfurnished lettings) | A |
| Interest on government stocks and foreign securities (not applicable to individuals) | C |
| Profits from a trade (eg builders) | D Case I |
| Profits from a profession (eg dentistry) | D Case II |
| Untaxed interest, annuities and other annual amounts received (eg National Savings Investment Account interest) | D Case III |
| Untaxed income arising from foreign possessions (eg foreign rents) | D Case IV |
| Any profits or gains not assessed under other schedules | D Case VI |
| Income from employment (eg wages or pensions) | E Cases I, II and III |
| Dividends and other distributions from UK resident companies (usually received net of tax) | F |

| Schedule and case | Basis of assessment | Normal due date of payment |
|---|---|---|
| A | Actual – rent due in the tax year, less allowable expenses | 1 January in tax year |
| C | Actual – received in the tax year | 1 December in next tax year |
| D Case I<br>D Case II | Preceding year basis – profits of accounting year ended in previous tax year | Equal instalments: 1 January in tax year and following 1 July |
| D Case III | Actual – where interest is received net of tax | Excess over basic rate: 1 December in next tax year |
| | Preceding year basis – where interest is received gross such as National Savings, bank interest | 1 January in tax year |
| D Case IV<br>    Case V | Preceding year basis | 1 January in tax year |
| E | Actual amount received | Normally through PAYE Scheme |
| F | Actual – dividends received plus accompanying tax credits | Excess over basic rate: 1 December in the next tax year |

It is neither appropriate nor feasible to explain the detailed operation of the various tax schedules in a book of this nature and it is proposed to confine the remainder of the explanation of our tax system to the business profits and tax of a dental practice.

Tax legislation does not define what expenses are allowable against profits for tax purposes but simply refers to them as 'wholly and necessarily' incurred in earning the profits. It is, therefore, left to the taxpayer and their advisers to negotiate with the Inspector of Taxes on contentious matters, if necessary involving the General Commissioners as adjudicators. However, some expenses are clearly tax deductible:

1   Materials used in extracting or restoring teeth.
2   Technician charges for making prosthetics.
3   Associate's remuneration.
4   Hygienist's remuneration.
5   Anaesthetist's fees.

6   Disposables (paper cups, napkins, mouthwash, etc.).
7   DSA salaries and national insurance.
8   Repairs to and maintenance of equipment (but not capital expenditure in replacing or upgrading it).
9   Replacement of hand instruments.
10   Rent (but not rent of owned property or domestic accommodation).
11   Rates, water, heating and lighting costs (except those relating to domestic accommodation).
12   Insurance and cleaning costs (relating to the business accommodation).
13   Property maintenance.
14   Reception salaries and NHI.
15   Telephone (business element).
16   Postage and carriage.
17   Professional stationery and printing.
18   Trade journals.
19   Waiting room magazines and technical books (except those used to learn the professional techniques, ie not textbooks).
20   Flowers for the waiting room and reception.
21   Bank charges and interest on practice bank account.
22   Professional subscriptions (GDC, MPS , MDU, BDA, etc.).
23   Advertising.
25   Staff uniforms and protective clothing.
24   Laundry of overalls, towels, etc.
26   Credit card service charges.
27   Radiological protection fees.
28   Staff canteen.
29   Staff Christmas Party (limited to £50 per head).
30   Motor expenses in connection with the practice but excluding travel from home and back.
31   Accountancy charges (concessionary) for preparing accounts but not for negotiating tax assessments.

Areas that are likely to give rise to argument are motor expenses (see also Chapter 17), the distinction between repairs and capital expenditure, private proportions of rent, heat and light, and cleaning. Most of these are subject to negotiation and depend upon individual circumstances.

## Basis of assessment

GDPs normally make up their accounts for a period of twelve months, and usually select when their year-end falls. Often it is best to have the first accounts covering a period of about a year, so that the financial year-end is fairly soon after 5 April. Under prevailing tax law, this ensures the greatest period between the time the profit is earned and the tax paid on it. The period covered by the accounts is known as the 'accounting year' and the tax year, ending on 5 April, is known as the 'fiscal year'.

Once a GDP has been operating for several years, the assessment in any fiscal year is based on the profits earned in the accounting year that ended in the preceding fiscal year. Thus the assessment for 1993/94 would be based on profit earned in the accounting year to 30 April 1992 as that ended during the fiscal year 1992/93. It also means that the tax would not actually be paid until 1 January and 1 July 1994 (in equal instalments).

However, where the year end is 31 March, the 1993/94 assessment would be based on profit made in the accounting year to 31 March 1993, which fell within the fiscal year 1992/93. This would leave nine months between the time the profit was earned and the tax paid, in the previous example it was 21 months.

## Commencement rules

For a new practice there are rules designed to enable the Inland Revenue to get onto the preceding year basis. Under these it is sometimes necessary to tax the same profit more than once.

There is a general belief that when a dentist sets up in practice they will not pay tax for three years. Unfortunately, this is a myth and the reality of the situation is simply that the tax bills may not arrive for that period – they then come in fairly quick succession and any GDP who believed they had a tax-free holiday will have a very grave shock.

Example: A GDP commenced in practice on 1 January 1991 and will make up accounts annually to 31 December. Profit for the year to 31 December:

1991 was £24,000

1992 was £32,000

1993 was £40,000

Assessments:

1990/91: actual profit for the period from 1 January to 5 April 1991 = 95/365 days at £24,000 = £6246.

1991/92: first 12 months profit: year to 31 December 1991 = £24,000

1991/92: previous year basis: profit for the year to 31 December 1992 = £24,000.

It will be seen that the first year's profit has been taxed three times and the total assessments amounted to £54,246. However, it is open to the taxpayer to elect to be taxed on an actual basis (under Section 62 ) in which case the assessments would be:

1990/91: unchanged at £6246.

1991/92: actual profit would be for the period 6 April 1991 to 5 April 1992 = (270/365 days at £24,000 plus 95/365 days at £32,000) = £26,083.

1992/93: actual profit would be for the period 6 April 1992 to 5 April 1993 = (270/365 days at £32,000 plus 95/365 days at £40,000) = £34,082.

This would mean that the total assessed to tax for the period would be £66,411. Quite obviously this is a much higher figure and the GDP would be foolish to make the election. However, there are instances in which it could be beneficial – usually when profits are falling – which, we hope, is unlikely in the case of a new dental practice.

Example: A GDP commenced in practice on 1 January 1991 and is making accounts up to 31 December annually. Profits are agreed as follows to the year ended 31 December:

1991 = £24,000

1992 = £15,000

1993 = £52,000

1994 = £48,000

On the normal basis the assessments would be:

1990/91: actual profit from 1 January to 5 April 1991: 95/365 days at £24,000 = £6246.

1991/92: first twelve months: 6 April 1991 to 6 April 1992 = £24,000.

1992/93: preceding year basis (ie year to 31 December 1992) = £24,000.

This gives total profits assessed over the three years as £54,246. However under Section 62 on an actual basis the assessments would be:

1990/91: unchanged at £6246.

1991/92: profit from 6 April 1991 to 5 April 1992 (270/365 days at £24,000 plus 95/365 days at £15,000) = £21,658.

1991/92: profit from 6 April 1992 to 5 April 1993 (270/365 days at £15,000 plus 95/365 × £52,000) = £24,630.

Under this method the total assessed profit would be £52,534 and obviously it would be sensible to adopt the election.

As always with tax law, there are time limits within which to make the Section 62 election. In this case the claim must be made within six years of the end of the third year of assessment (in this case by 5 April 1999). Alternatively, if the election is to be revoked the same time limit applies. The first and fourth years would remain the same irrespective of the election.

# Change of accounting period

At one time it was possible to save tax by changing the financial year-end, but the Inland Revenue has become wise to this practice and it is now exceedingly difficult to benefit from a change of year-end.

Example: A GDP has for some years made accounts up to 31 March but has now decided to change to 30 June. Profits are agreed as follows to:

| | | |
|---|---|---|
| year to 31 March | 1990 | £35,000 |
| | 1991 | £42,000 |
| 15 months to 30 June | 1992 | £55,000 |

1993/94: this assessment is based on the profits to 30 June 1992: $12/15 \times £55,000 = £44,000$.

1992/93: there is no accounting period to form this year's assessment and consequently the Inland Revenue will take 12 months to the new accounting year end: $9/12 \times £42,000$ plus $3/15 \times £55,000 = £42,500$.

1991/92: the original assessment would be based on the year to 31 March 1991: £42,000. However, the Inland Revenue may have the assessment adjusted to profit for the period to 30 June 1990: $9/12 \times £35,000$ plus $3/12 \times £42,000 = £36,750$

The 'averaging principle' is then applied in order to ascertain whether the period 1991/92 has been over- or under-assessed:

| | | |
|---|---|---|
| 12 months to 31 March | 1990 | £35,000 |
| | 1991 | £42,000 |
| 15 months to 30 June | 1992 | £55,000 |
| | | ———— |
| Total | | £132,000 |

Profit to be assessed over 4 years = 48/39 × £132,000 = £162,462. Profit is actually fixed at:

1990/91 = £35,000

1992/93 = £42,500

1993/94 = £44,000

Total = £121,500. This leaves £40,962 (ie £162,462 less £121,500) to assess in 1991/92. The assessment for 1991/92 will only be altered if there is a material difference.   There is a material difference if :

1   The averaging of the current and preceding years assessment (1991/92 and 1990/91 on the original basis) is less than 10%,
2   The difference is less than £1000.

In this case the difference between £40,962 and £42,000 is more than £1000. The assessment for 1991/92 will be reduced to £40,692. Thus the revised assessments are:

1990/91 = £35,000

1991/92 = £40,962

1992/93 = £42,500

1993/94 = £44,000

## Cessation provisions

Whilst a GDP has election rights when they commence in practice, the choice in the closing years lies with the Inland Revenue. The final three years of assessment will be subject to revision.
   When a GDP ceases trading the Inland Revenue cannot tax the GDP beyond the cessation date. As indicated in Chapter 15, the years of assessment are based on the preceding year basis, also, certain profits may have been taxed twice in the opening periods. Therefore when a GDP ceases trading, certain profits will not be taxed.

### Assessments

Example: A GDP has been in business for many years and retired on 30 June, 1993. Profit for the year ended 31 December:

1989 was £44,500

1990 was £46,000

1991 was £51,000

1992 was £56,000

6 months to 30 June 1993 was £24,000

*Original assessments*

Year of assessment:

| | | | |
|---|---|---|---|
| 1993/94 | Actual 6.4.93 to 30.6.93: | | |
| | ³⁄₆ × £24,000 | | £12,000 |
| 1992/93 | PYB YE 31.12.91 | £51,000 | |
| 1991/92 | PYB YE 31.12.90 | £46,000 | |
| 1990/91 | PYB YE 31.12.89 | | |
| | (unchanged) | | £44,500 |
| | Total | £97,000 | |

*Revised assessments*

Under Section 63 Taxes Act 1988 the Inland Revenue will have the option to revise the assessments as follows :

Year of assessment:

| | | | |
|---|---|---|---|
| 1993/94 | as before | | £12,000 |
| 1992/93 | actual 6.4.92 to 5.4.93: | | |
| | ³⁄₆ × £24,000 + ⁹⁄₁₂ × £56,000 | £54,000 | |
| 1991/92 | actual 6.4.91 to 5.4.92: | | |
| | ³⁄₁₂ × £56,000 + ⁹⁄₁₂ × £51,000 | £52,250 | |
| 1990/91 | unchanged | | £44,500 |
| | Total | £106,250 | |

As the revised assessment under Section 63 will result in larger taxable profits, the Inland Revenue will take the option to amend the 1991/92 and 1992/93 assessments.

Planning for retirement is, therefore, essential. If this GDP were to reduce their income in the final three years, then the penultimate and ante-penultimate year of assessments would not be amended, thereby incurring no additional income tax charges.

# 16

# Capital allowance

Capital allowances are a substitute for depreciation. For accounting purposes depreciation is usually taken at 25% of cost of the asset or of the book value at commencement of the accounting period. For tax purposes this has to be added back to the profit and replaced with a standard capital allowance, which has been steadily reduced by government to the present levels.

There are various categories of capital allowances, each with its own rules, but usually a GDP will be concerned only with plant and equipment and with motor vehicles.

## Plant and equipment

Tax law does not define plant and machinery and it has been left to the Courts to decide in individual instances. In Yarmouth $v$ France (1887) it was said that:

'. . . (it) includes whatever apparatus is used by a business man for carrying on his business – not his stock in trade which he buys or makes for sale but all goods and chattels, fixed or moveable, live or dead, which he keeps for permanent employment in his business.'

In a dental practice this will almost certainly include all the dental and office equipment, waiting room furniture and furnishings, and will also extend to such items as demountable partitioning, cabinets and the reception counter. It is unlikely that an Inspector of Taxes would insist upon hand instruments being capitalized but is more likely to allow replacements to be charged as an operating expense. The equipment is likely to be pooled together under the heading of plant and equipment.

# Writing down allowance (WDA)

In calculating capital allowances the Inland Revenue will use a fixed rate of 25% on cost or on the written down value (WDV) at commencement of the basis period.

Example: A dentist has been in practice for several years and has made accounts up to 30 April. At 5 April 1993 the WDV of the equipment is £3,000 and in the year to 30 April 1992 the following capital purchases were made:

| | | |
|---|---|---|
| 1 June 1991 | chair | £15,000 |
| 21 December 1991 | X-ray | £5,000 |
| 5 April 1992 | cabinetry | £1,000 |
| Total | | £21,000 |

| | Pool | Claim |
|---|---|---|
| WDV at 6 April 1992 | £3,000 | |
| Additions | £21,000 | |
| | £24,000 | |
| WDA at 25% | £6,000 | £6,000 |
| WDA at 5.4.94 | £18,000 | |

Capital allowances for the year 1993/94 = £6,000. The expenditure was incurred in 1991/92 but allowance is not received until 1993/94, which reflects the preceding year basis in assessment of business profits for tax purposes.

The exact date of a purchase will often be vitally important, more so in the last two years preceding cessation of a business. It is also essential to bear in mind that if a dentist is given in excess of 4 months credit by a supplier, the expenditure will be deemed to have been incurred at the point of payment.

# Balancing charges

A balancing charge (BC) will occur when the sale proceeds of the asset exceeds the written down value for tax purposes.

Example: An asset with a WDV at 6 April 1994 of £9,000 was sold for £15,000. It was replaced with a similar item costing £12,000. The tax allowances are as follows:

|                | Pool     |
|----------------|----------|
|                | Pool     |
| WDV at 6.4.94  | £9,000   |
| Sale proceeds  | £15,000  |
|                |          |
| BC             | £6,000   |
|                |          |
| Addition       | £12,000  |
| WDA at 25%     | £3,000   |
|                |          |
| WDV at 5.4.95  | £9,000   |

This will mean that the capital allowances will be balancing charge £6000 less WDA £3,000 = £3,000 added to the taxable profit. It is very important to realize that any balancing charge arising on sale of equipment (or any other asset) will be added to the taxable profit and brought into charge for income tax at the highest rate.

# Balancing allowance

Where an asset is sold for less than the WDV the shortfall qualifies as a balancing allowance, which can be deducted from the business profits, thereby qualifying for tax relief. It cannot be claimed in addition to WDA for that year on the same asset.

Example: If a GDP sells equipment for £5,000 at a time when the WDV was £8,000, they will qualify for a balancing allowance of £3,000; they would also be unable to claim £2,000 WDA.

# Selling a practice

It is essential in selling a practice to ensure that the apportionment of sale proceeds will be less than the WDV of the asset. However, as the purchaser will be looking for a much higher value on equipment to gain capital allowances, it is often necessary to reach a compromise settlement, although it is important to bear in mind that an astute HMIT may well ask for details of how the apportionment was reached and will perhaps ask for a list of the individual items of equipment included in the sale.

# 17

# Motor cars

Like most professionals, dentists tend to purchase expensive motor vehicles, which they feel can be run on the practice, a view that is justified by the claim to its use for domicilary visits and other professional journeys.

The amount that the accountant is able to negotiate by way of a disallowance for personal use of the vehicle will depend on individual circumstances and the attitude of the local Inspector of Taxes. Indeed, it is usually only when there is an 'in-depth' investigation that the matter comes to a head and a realistic proportion is renegotiated.

The Inland Revenue is always, of course, entitled to rely upon the strict wording of the law – that expenditure must be 'wholly necessarily and exclusively' for the business. It was decided in the case of Sergeant *v* Barnes that the whole of the motor expenses can be disallowed where there is a dual purpose. In that case, travelling from home to surgery and back but calling at the laboratory en route. In reality, however, the Inland Revenue will seek to establish a fair proportion of expenditure for business use and restrict the tax deduction to that sum.

In order to establish the situation beyond doubt, the practitioner should ideally maintain a log book showing individual journeys, the relevant mileage and the purpose of the trip. By this means there will be adequate evidence to challenge the Inspector of Taxes who is seeking to disallow an unduly large portion of expenditure.

Not only does the negotiated disallowance relate to running costs such as petrol, maintenance, licence and insurance but also to capital expenditure.

Example:

| | Car No. 1 | Car No. 2 |
|---|---|---|
| Cost of car | £6,500 | |
| Writing down allowance – 25% | £1,625 | |
| | £4,875 | |
| Sale proceeds | £4,000 | |
| Balancing charge | £875 | |
| Addition | | £15,000 |
| Writing down allowance – restricted | | £3,000 |
| Carried forward | | £12,000 |

In the case of car no. 1 the allowance is 25% of cost or balance at beginning of the year. On disposal of the car the deficit on sale is treated as wholly allowable. In the case of car no. 2 the allowance is 25% of cost or £3000, whichever is the lower (for cars purchased after 10 March 1992). In each case the writing down allowance of balancing charge is restricted to the agreed business percentage of motor expenses.

The situation with leasing is identical in that a portion will be disallowed for private use, as is the case with hire purchase charges.

# 18

# Capital gains tax

Capital gains tax (CGT) was introduced in the Finance Act (1965) and arises on the disposal of any chargeable asset, business or private:

1   Freehold or leasehold properties.
2   Goodwill.
3   Stocks and shares.
4   Intangible assets such as copyright, trade marks, etc.
5   Any currency other than sterling.

Before it was introduced only profits that fell into the category of trading fell into charge for tax, and this gave rise to many arguments over what did or did not constitute trading. After its introduction, the main criticism of CGT was the fact that it did not allow for inflationary gains; between 1965 and 1982, for example, roughly half of the gain was due to inflation. In March 1982 the government introduced legislation to rectify this anomaly. Indexation relief was geared to the RPI (Retail Price Index) and affected all gains after 1982/83. A further refinement of the law in 1988 assumed that all assets were held in March 1982, which means that for any assets owned prior to that date the owner will need to determine its value on 15 March 1982 when the eventual gain comes to be computed.

CGT is quite distinct from income tax and consequently losses incurred in trading cannot be offset against a chargeable gain or vice versa, with one exception. In the actual year of the gain being realized any trading loss can be offset. However as few GDPs would find themselves in such a situation, the point is somewhat academic.

The tax is payable on 1 December in the fiscal year following that in which the gain was realized. Thus, a gain made in March 1993 will fall due for payment on 1 December 1993.

There are circumstances where a chargeable gain can arise even though no money was received for the asset and this can create hardship.

# Rate of capital gains tax

The rate of CGT is charged at the individual taxpayer's marginal rate. For example, if a GDP's income is charged at 40% income tax the CGT will be levied at the same rate.

Example: A GDP has a chargeable gain of £10,000 and an income of £26,000.

| | | |
|---|---|---|
| Profit | | £26,000 |
| Personal allowances | £3,445 | |
| Class IV National Insurance | £471 | |
| Superannuation | £2,000 | |
| | | £5,916 |
| Tax chargeable on | | £20,084 |

Chargeable: £20,084 at basic rate leaving £3616 of basic rate uncovered

| | | |
|---|---|---|
| CGT: chargeable gain | £10,000 | |
| Annual exemption | £5,500 | |
| Chargeable | £4,500 | |
| £3616 at 25% = £904 | | |
| £884 at 40% = £353.60 | | |
| CGT payable | £1,257.60 | |

# Reliefs

In calculating CGT it is permissible to deduct expenses arising in connection with the acquisition and disposal. In addition there are the following reliefs:

1   An allowance of £5800 annual exemption per person (but this is not allowed where 'roll-over' relief is claimed nor is it available in addition to retirement or sickness allowance.
2   The individual's main residence is exempt from a gain, as are disposals between husband and wife.
3   Retirement relief is available to an individual 55 years or over.  The allowance is £150,000 plus 50% of the gain between £150,000 and £600,000, which effectively means a maximum of £375,000. This applies from 18 March 1991.
4   In the event of retirement through ill-health the taxpayer may claim retirement relief but must obtain a special form of medical certificate through their FHSA.

It is worthwhile noting that:

1   Attempts to break down the chargeable gain into different years for the purpose of avoiding CGT are unlikely to be successful because the Inland Revenue has the right to treat them as connected gains.
2   Retirement means precisely that – it is not comparable with the 24-hour retirement for pension purposes.
3   Property values (including the value at 15 March 1982) are agreed with the District Valuer, who may substitute a figure; there is an appeal process.
4   CGT does not apply to dental equipment and fixtures; these items fall within the scope of capital allowances and consequently will be chargeable to a balancing charge or rank for a balancing allowance depending on the sale proceeds.
5   A motor vehicle intended to run on the road is exempt from CGT. It will only fall within the scope of capital allowances if it has been claimed as a business asset for tax purposes.

Where an asset is held jointly by husband and wife, it may be worthwhile considering transfer of the whole to the husband (or wife) prior to sale in order to gain retirement or sickness relief. This is, however, an area which requires proper professional guidance.

# Roll-over relief

When a GDP sells their practice there will be a charge to CGT unless they have reached retirement age (55 plus) or are withdrawing due to ill health. If, however, the GDP chooses to reinvest the whole of the proceeds in a new practice (or other business) within three years they may claim 'roll-over' of the chargeable gain onto the new assets. The effect is, of course, simply to delay the gain until retirement but it can nevertheless be beneficial.

Roll-over relief only applies to business assets and not to disposal of shares or investment property (the taxpayer is entitled to have one main residence exempt from CGT). The broad groups are:

1 Land and buildings used wholly for business purposes.
2 Goodwill.
3 Ships, aircraft, hovercraft.
4 Milk quotas.
5 Furnished holiday lettings.

Furnished holiday letting property must be available for letting to the public for at least 140 days during the year and must actually be let for 70. The same person cannot occupy it for more than 31 consecutive days in a period of at least seven months. This test is rigidly applied by HMIT.

## Number of applications

Roll-over relief can be applied an indefinite number of times although, in reality, the point will be reached where it is no longer viable. The replacement asset has to be purchased within 3 years of realisation of the gain although it can be 'rolled back' for up to 12 months prior to realisation.

Example: A property is sold for £300,000 but has an outstanding mortgage of £160,000. Effectively the GDP will receive only £140,000. However, roll-over relief only arises if the full £300,000 is reinvested. The fact that part of the proceeds is needed to clear the mortgage is irrelevant.

## How does roll-over relief work in practice?

Example: A GDP sells their practice for £230,000 in April 1992. It was purchased for £150,000 in December 1986. The sale proceeds includes equipment valued at £10,000 and the original purchase included £15,000 for equipment. The replacement practice costs £290,000, which includes £20,000 for equipment.

| | | |
|---|---:|---:|
| Sale proceeds (excluding equipment) | | £220,000 |
| Cost (excluding equipment) | £140,000 | |
| Legal fees on acquisition and disposal (including agents) | £4800 | |
| | £144,800 | £144,800 |
| | | £75,200 |
| Indexation Allowance £140,000 × 0.393 (note equipment and legal costs are not indexed) | | £55,020 |
| Roll-over gain | | £20,180 |

The proceeds (£220,000) were wholly 'rolled over' onto the new practice (£270,000 excluding equipment).

If a GDP has purchased a new practice before selling the existing one, roll-over of the gain is still possible provided the sale takes place within 12 months of the acquisition. The reinvestment has to be for wholly business purposes and one of the assets listed in the Act. It is also important to note that the entire proceeds have to be reinvested to qualify.

Calculation of the CGT is related to the actual disposal value and does not allow for deduction of mortgage repayment. This point often causes confusion and individuals feel it unfair that they cannot clear the mortgage from the proceeds of sale before reinvesting.

Example: In July 1992 the new practice will be valued for CGT purposes at £270,000 less the roll-over gain of £20,180 = £249,820. It is this figure that will be treated as the 'acquisition price' and indexed for the purpose of computing the gain when it too is sold.

# Part reinvestment

If only part of the sale proceeds are reinvested then cash will be available to pay CGT and, therefore, only part of the gain will qualify for relief.

Example: A GDP sold a practice in December 1992 for £260,000. The practice had been purchased for £80,000 in June 1983. A new practice was purchased for £210,000:

| Capital gains tax computation: 1992/93 | |
|---|---:|
| Sale proceeds | £260,000 |
| Less: Cost | £80,000 |
| | £180,000 |
| Less: indexation allowance (0.641 × £80,000) | £51,280 |
| Chargeable gain | £128,720 |
| Part not reinvested (£260,000 − £210,000 ) | £50,000 |
| Roll-over relief | £78,720 |
| | £128,720 |

The £50,000 will be chargeable to CGT. The base cost of new practice is (£210,000 less £78,720) = £131,280

# Part replacement

There are two occasions where roll-over relief will not apply:

1 Where only part of the sale proceeds are not reinvested.
2 Where the reinvestment is in a depreciating asset.

# Depreciating assets

An example of a depreciating asset is a leasehold property. Roll-over relief is substituted by hold-over relief, in which case the chargeable gain on the old asset will become chargeable to CGT at the earliest of the following events:

1   The disposal of the replacement asset.
2   The date it ceases to be used in the business.
3   Ten years after its purchase.

If the asset is replaced the roll-over relief will apply to the further replacement asset.

# Retirement relief

The conditions given on retirement relief have been explained briefly earlier in this chapter.

If the gain is less than £150,000 full relief is available.

If the gain is between £150,000 and £600,000 the relief available is £150,000 + half of the excess over £150,000.

If the gain is over £600,000 the relief available is the maximum = £375,000 (ie £150,000 + 0.5 (£600,000 − £150,000)).

To qualify for retirement relief the assets disposed of must be a business asset (ie property, goodwill, etc.) and have been used in business for at least 10 years. The relief will be reduced on a sliding scale if the conditions are not met. This ranges from 10% to 100%. There are other aspects for retirement relief such as disposal of shares held in the family company, but no attempt is made here to demonstrate this, as it has no relevance to a dental practice.

# 19

# Inheritance tax

Originally known as 'death duties', inheritance tax dates back to 1964. Inheritance Tax today covers not only an individual's estate passing on death but also on gifts made within 7 years prior to death.

## Exemptions

Transfer of assets or value between husband and wife are always exempt but there are other transfers which, provided they comply with the appropriate rules, are also exempt from inheritance tax:

1   Gifts to registered charities.
2   Gifts and bequests to political parties.
3   Gifts for national purposes (eg to the National Gallery, the National Trust, British Museum, etc.).
4   Gifts for public benefit (eg land and buildings of special interest, works of art, etc.).
5   Gifts up to the value of £3000 in any year.
6   Gifts of up to £250 per donee in any tax year.

## Inheritance tax planning

Inheritance tax planning is essential where an individual has accumulated a large estate. There are a number of ways in which the tax can be avoided.

### Transfer of property during lifetime

This will attract tax at 0% up to £150,000 and 20% thereafter. However, if the donor survives for seven years the value transferred will become exempt. These are known as PETs (potentially exempt transfers). The value is taken at the date of transfer and not at the date of death, by which time the asset may well have appreciated in value. However, if it has depreciated, it may be possible to adjust the duty. Where the donor does not survive for seven years the rate of inheritance tax will be abated:

| Year before death | % of inheritance tax |
|---|---|
| 0-3 | 100 |
| 3-4 | 80 |
| 4-5 | 60 |
| 5-6 | 40 |
| 6+ | 20 |

Example: The history of a GDP's transfer of assets to his grandsons were as follows:

Gift A: March 1989: £160,000
Gift B: March 1991: £50,000
In September 1993 he died with an estate valued at £150,000.

Gift A was originally a PET but becomes chargeable on death. As the gift was between 4 and 5 years prior to death the inheritance tax is chargeable at 60% of the death rate:

| £160,000 at 40% | £64,000 |
|---|---|
| Payable: 60% of £64,000 | £38,400 |

Gift B was within three years and the full death rate is payable:

£160,000 + £50,000 = £210,000

| First £150,000 | nil |
|---|---|
| £60,000 at 40% | £24,000 |
| As above | £38,400 |
| | |
| Payable in full | £62,400 |
| Payable on death: | |
| £150,000 at 40% | £60,000 |

### Transfer of property up to a limit

Inheritance tax can be saved by one spouse leaving property up to the value of £150,000 to the children (this will be within the exemption limit) and the rest to the spouse (which is also exempt). The surviving spouse can later leave £150,000 to the children exempt of inheritance tax. However, it is wise to bear in mind the problems with family breakdown.

## Payment of inheritance tax

Inheritance tax is payable when the Estate is submitted with the probate application. On certain assets (eg property) the duty can be deferred by six months after which interest accumulates.

In the case of lifetime transfers between 6 April and 30 September the duty is payable on the following 30 April; for those between 1 October and 5 April the tax is payable six months after the end of the fiscal year of transfer. The Personal Representative (or Executor) will usually pay the duty before probate is granted. In certain cases the Personal Representative does not have the funds or access to them until after Probate is granted; in such instances there are provisions for the tax to be paid by ten equal annual payments.

# 20

# Dental health schemes

Over the years there have been many attempts to establish Dental Health Insurance Schemes but these have not been successful due mainly to the difficulty in establishing the difference between what is clinically necessary and cosmetically desirable.

Several schemes, which were somewhat different in nature, were established in 1986, some survived and others failed for a variety of reasons. Today the leading capitation based scheme is Denplan Limited, now part of PPP, and its green apple logo is now to be seen in practices throughout the UK.

Denplan boasts that it currently has about 25% of practising dentists on its lists, and roughly one-third of a million patients.

A patient that a GDP is proposing to take on as a Denplan patient will be examined and allocated to a payment category. There are five groups and the national average fees are:

Group A          £6.21 per month

Group B          £9.32 per month

Group C          £11.55 per month

Group D          £16.21 per month

Group E          £19.64 per month

About three-quarters of patients fall into Group C.

Denplan collects the monthly payments from the patient's bank account by direct debit and, after deducting its administrative costs, will remit the GDP's share with a schedule of patients on a monthly basis, the payment covers check-ups, consultations, scale and polish and X-rays. Practitioner's time for crown and bridge work is covered but the patient still has to pay the laboratory charge. Patients have insurance cover for trauma and there is a payment made for emergency treatment away from home.

The scheme is popular with GDPs because it offers a regular monthly income and patients tend to find it an easy way of budgeting for their dental treatment. However, some patients react against the scheme because they do not perceive it as being profitable to them to make the monthly payment. Likewise, some dentists are of the opinion that the costs of operating the system are high and that an equivalent service can be offered 'in-house', although this does involve the practice staff in additional paperwork. At the time of writing, BUPA have recently entered the dental market and launched BUPA Dental Cover, which offers a similar package to the Denplan/PPP scheme. Practitioners seeking BUPA registration must however first undergo a practice inspection.

There are arguments for and against capitation based schemes. The concerns focus on supervised neglect as a result of under prescription, and these must be addressed by the leading players in the dental market to protect the long-term credibility of these schemes. On balance, it is likely that they will continue to grow as an increasing number of practitioners opt out of the NHS.

# 21

# National insurance contributions

Generally speaking everyone working in the UK is liable to pay national insurance contributions.

## Class 1: employed persons national insurance

This is deducted from an employee's salary by the employer, who remits the payment to the Inland Revenue on a monthly basis:

*Employee's national insurance*

Employees earning up to £54 per week pay 2% of that amount in national insurance; employees earning between £54.01 and £405 pay 9% national insurance. The monthly figures are £234 and £1755, respectively.

*Employer's national insurance*

Earnings:

| | |
|---|---|
| £54 to £89.99 | 4.6% |
| £90 to £134.99 | 6.6% |
| £135 to £189.99 | 8.6% |
| Thereafter (no upper limit) | 10.4% |

## Contracted out

*Employee's national insurance*

| | |
|---|---|
| On the first £54 per week | 2% |
| Thereafter (up to £405) | 7% |

*Employer's national insurance*

Earnings:

| | |
|---|---|
| £54 to £89.99 | 4.6% on the first £54; 0.08% thereafter |
| £90 to £134.99 | 6.6% on the first £54; 2.8% thereafter |
| £135 to £189.99 | 8.6% on the first £54; 4.8% thereafter |
| £190 to £405 | 10.4% on the first £54; 6.6% thereafter |
| Over £405 | 10.4% |

There is a reduced rate for married women and widows, with a valid certificate of election, of 3.85% up to £405 but the employer's contributions are unchanged.

Men over 65 and women over 60 years do not pay national insurance, although the employer's contributions are unchanged.

Children under 16 years do not pay national insurance.

## Class 2

The self-employed pay a flat rate of £5.35 per week although there is a small earnings exception on incomes up to £3030 per annum.

## Class 3

These are voluntary contributions of £5.25 per week; they are not mandatory. The only reason for paying them would be to preserve benefits.

## Class 4

This is an additional charge on the self-employed and is collected with the annual Schedule D tax. It is calculated at 6.3% of income between £6120 and £21,060 per annum. If the individual reaches pensionable age at the beginning of the year of assessment there is no liability.

# Benefits

## Statutory maternity pay

Ninety per cent of the employee's average weekly earnings with a lower rate of £46.30 per week for 18 weeks.

## Statutory sick pay (SSP)

Nothing paid for earnings under £54 per week. For earnings of between £54 and £189.99 per week, SSP is paid at the rate of £45.30 per week and for earnings of over £190 it is paid at the standard rate of £52.50.

## Retirement pensions

*Single person*

The single person's pension is £54.15 per week

*Married couples*

Where both made national insurance contributions, both will receive £54.15 per week each but where the wife was not a contributor she will be paid £32.55 per week. There is an age addition of 25p per week for persons over 80 years.

## Hospital downrating

£10.85 per week

## Widow's Benefit and widowed mothers allowance

£54.15 per week

## Non-contributory pension

| | |
|---|---|
| Single person (category C or D) | £2.55 per week |
| Married couple (category C) | £52 per week |

Married couple (category D — 80 and over)     £65.10 per week

Age addition                                                      25p per week

## Invalidity allowance

The lower, middle and higher rates of invalidity are £3.60, £7.20 and £11.55 per week, respectively.

## Invalid care allowance

Each qualifying individual £32.55 per week with an earnings limit of £40. There is an adult dependency increase of £19.45 per week.

## Unemployment benefit

This is £43.10 per week under pension age; with additions of £26.60 for each dependent adult. For someone over retirement age these figures are £54.15 and £32.55 per week, respectively. Child dependency is £9.75 per week for a child for whom higher rate child benefit is paid and £10.85 for others.

## Attendance allowance

The lower rate is £28.95; the higher rate is £43.35 per week.

## Child benefit

£9.65 per week is paid for the eldest child and £7.80 paid for all other children.

## Disability living allowance

The care component is £11.55, £28.95 or £43.35 per week. The mobility component is £11.55 or £30.30 per week

## One parent families

£5.85 per week is given in addition to child benefit for the first or only child of a single person

## Maternity allowance

This is £42.25 per week

## Widow's payment

This is £1000.

# Tax

Some allowances are taxable under Schedule E:

1   Income support payments to unemployed strikers.
2   Industrial death benefit.
3   Invalid care allowance.
4   Invalidity allowance paid with a retirement pension.
5   Job release allowances.
6   Non-contributory retirement pension.
7   Retirement pension.
8   Statutory maternity pay.
9   Statutory sick pay.
10   Unemployment benefit.
11   Widowed mother's allowance.
12   Widow's pension.

Other benefits are tax free:

1   Maternity allowance.
2   Sickness benefit.
3   Child benefit.
4   Child dependency additions paid with widow's pension, widowed mother's allowance, retirement pension or invalid care allowance.
5   Guardian's allowance.
6   One parent benefit.
7   Constant attendance allowance.
8   Industrial injuries disablement benefit.
9   Attendance allowance.

10   Christmas bonus.
11   Community care benefit.
12   Disability living allowance.
13   Family benefit.
14   Housing benefit.
15   Job release allowance to women of 59 and men of 64.
16   Mobility allowance.
17   Redundancy payment.
18   Widow's payment.

A person who receives income from more than one source (eg self-employment and employment) will be required to pay both Class 2 and Class 4 national insurance contributions. However there are limits to the maximum amount of national insurance contributions.

For Class 1 National Insurance contributions the maximum amount will be (1992/93):

£54 at 2% + (£54 − £405) @ 9% × 53 weeks = £1731.51

Class 1 and Class 2 contributions must not exceed £1731.51.

Example: A GDP earns £250 per week and is also self-employed:

Class 1: 52 × (£54 @ 2%) + (£54 − £250) @ 9%      £973.44
Class 2: 52 × £5.35                                                      £278.20
                                                                              ─────────
                                                                              £1251.64

A deferment of Class 4 contributions will need to be notified to the Department of Social Security, preferably before the beginning of the tax year, otherwise before the 15 February in the tax year. Remember, if the maximum amount is reached there will be no need to pay Class 4 National Insurance contributions.

Patients in receipt of unemployment benefit or retirement  pensions are entitled to free dental treatment.

# Superannuation and pensions

Until comparatively recently NHS dentists were obliged to contribute 6% of their superannuable earnings to the Department of Social Security (DSS) superannuation scheme. It is now possible to opt out of the DSS scheme, although this may be somewhat unwise because it is far superior to any private pension plan.

## The DSS scheme

Under the DSS scheme a GDP contributes 6% of superannuable earnings, with the balance being added by the Department of Health. At the normal retirement age of 65 (males) or 60 (females) there will be a tax-free lump sum followed by an index-linked pension for life (linked to the Retail Price Index). The pension is calculated on the years of superannuable service multiplied by 1/80th of the final salary.

However, as the majority of GDPs will achieve their peak earnings relatively early their career, it is likely that, when they draw their pension, they will be worse off than a dentist in hospital service and accordingly there is provision to compensate the GDP. The lump sum and pension will be calculated on average total career earnings uprated by a dynamising factor, which adjusts for the effect of inflation. This is multiplied by 1.4%.

Example: A dentist whose average dynamized Superannuation (SA) was £64,000 after 38 years service will receive an annual pension of £64,000 × 38 × 1.4% = £34,048 plus a tax free lump sum of (3 × £34,048) = £102,144.

## Death in service

In a case where the GDP dies before retirement, the benefits would be:

1 Death gratuity, which is roughly equivalent to one year's superannuable pay.

2  A widow's index-linked pension equivalent to 50% of the pension the GDP would have received at the date of death.

3  Where the GDP is survived by at least one child under the age of 17 years in full-time education an additional pension of between 25% and 50% of the widow's pension. There are special provisions where no parent survives.

Unless there has been an election to purchase pension benefits for the pre-April 1988 period, the widower of a female GDP will receive a pension based on service from April 1988 only.

# Death after retirement

Once the GDP has commenced drawing their pension, on death their spouse will receive 50% of the pension for life, plus an additional pension of between 25% and 50% whilst a child of the marriage is under the age of 17 years and in full-time education.

# Ill-health retirement

Provided the GDP has at least two years pensionable service they will be entitled to a lump sum and pension on retirement through ill health. In this case the payments are based on the actual number of years in reckonable service enhanced with up to six years and 243 days in the case of someone who has at least ten years service and a lower enhancement for less.

# Tax

Contributions to the DSS scheme are allowable for tax purposes at the highest rate of tax paid. Thus a taxpayer chargeable to tax at higher band rate would get 40% tax relief on the 6% contributions to the DSS superannuation. However, if they choose to do so, they may elect to forego this tax relief under Extra Statutory Concession A9 and thereby qualify for full tax relief on payments into a private pension plan.

## Private pension plans

GDPs have always been entitled to contribute into a private pension scheme on their NRE (net relevant earnings) from private dentistry; they could extend this to cover the NHS earnings by electing to forego relief on the DSS superannuation (see above). The tax relief on payments into a private pension plan are limited to between 17% and 40% of NRE as follows:

| Age at beginning of tax year | Maximum contribution |
|---|---|
| 35 and under | 17.5% |
| 36 to 45 | 20% |
| 46 to 50 | 25% |
| 51 to 55 | 30% |
| 56 to 60 | 35% |
| 61 years and over | 40% |

## Additional voluntary contributions

Added years can be purchased in the form of additional voluntary contributions (AVCs) to the DSS scheme; or a private pension plan can be set up to operate alongside the NHS scheme.

## Opting out of the NHS

GDPs who have chosen to opt out of NHS dentistry, ought really to consider making alternative provisions for a private pension plan to replace the DSS scheme. Benefits are likely to be less attractive but there are certain advantages:

1   A private pension can usually be drawn at 50.
2   It may either be taken as a pension or as a tax-free lump sum with a reduced pension.
3   Retirement is not a pre-requisite to drawing the pension; the retirement can, therefore, be phased over a period of time.

4   Sometimes the lump sum can be assigned as collateral for a mortgage, which means that the mortgage will be interest-only, the capital debt being cleared by the lump sum payment. It is, however, wise to bear in mind that there has been a great deal of discussion recently about taxing the lump sum payment and, if this legislation is passed and is retrospective (which it could be, although we do not have a policy of retrospective legislation in the UK), this could present difficulties in clearing a mortgage on retirement.

GDPs taking their pension in the private sector will need to give some thought to life assurance to replace the death in service cover, and should also consider permanent health insurance to replace sickness/disability cover. Whilst this can be costly and will increase with age, it does ensure a guaranteed income (possibly index-linked) up to the age of 60. The premium can be reduced where the GDP is prepared to wait one month, three months or six months before taking benefit under the insurance.

## Staff pensions

It is possible to effect a pension for employees, and for the GDP's spouse if they work in the practice. In the case of employees this can be a reward for service; in the case of the spouse it gives a further lump sum and life-long pension, which can be especially helpful where the GDP dies first. All the premiums are deductible for tax purposes.

## Advice

Practitioners would be well advised to seek independent advice on their pension arrangements where they are considering investment outside the DSS scheme. Where they are contracted with a dental health scheme, it is likely that the body concerned will have its own arrangements which need to be considered carefully.

# 23

# Value-added tax (VAT)

Dentistry is exempt for VAT purposes, which means that a GDP cannot register as a VAT trader in relation to their profession; this has been the case since VAT was introduced in 1971. However, there have been changes in relation to the partial exemption rules in the last two years and it is now easier for GDPs to register in connection with their chargeable sales, which may be:

1  Sale of toothbrushes, floss or other supplies.
2  Sale of tea or coffee in the waiting room.
3  Provision of a payphone for the use of patients.

There are two schools of thought as to whether a GDP should register for VAT purposes:

1  There are those dentists (and their advisers) who see VAT registration as a means of releasing further income for the practice.
2  There are those who see the paperwork and problems that can follow as creating their own problems at a time when GDPs are seeking to minimize their paperwork.

## VAT registration

To register as a VAT trader it is necessary to make taxable supplies, which must fall into one of the above categories. A form VAT1 will then need to be submitted to the local VAT office which will process the registration and allocate a VAT number. Once registered it is necessary to remain in the system for at least 12 months.

# Quarterly returns

Each registered trader is allocated a 'stagger' period which means that the first quarterly return will be received between two and five months after the date of registration; thereafter they will be received quarterly. Shortly before the end of a quarter the trader will be sent a VAT quarterly return and they have one calendar month from the end of the quarter in which to complete and submit it to the VAT Central Control Unit at Southend. There are penalties for late submission of returns or payment of VAT. The tax is collected on this self-assessment basis.

# Records

It is necessary to maintain a detailed record of sales and also a record of all payments made showing the VAT paid on supplies. Such records have to be retained for a period of six years. As GDPs will not actively add VAT to their sales, it will be assumed that the revenue is VAT inclusive, which means that it can be calculated on the basis of 17.5/117.5 of the VATable sales.  If, therefore, the GDP has sold toothbrushes worth £145 during the quarter, they are due to account for output tax of £21.60.

The GDP is entitled to claw back input tax, the amount of which will depend on the taxable purchases. In the average dental practice the materials are likely to be in the region of £3000 per annum, and there may be some other taxable items, such as telephone, stationery and motor expenses. If it is assumed that in the quarter these will amount to £3500 there will be a reclaim for £521.28. The trader will be repaid the net sum of £499.68. The amount of any potential repayment will, of course, be very much higher where there are capital purchases of equipment during the quarter.

However, the *de minimus* rule applies, which means that the amount that can be repaid in any quarter will not exceed £1900 and, if the repayment works out at more than this sum, nothing will be repaid, although the GDP will still have to pay input tax less the output tax on the taxable items being sold.

# Is VAT worthwhile?

The problem is that any VAT repayment is, of course, subject to normal income tax because it enhances the practice profits. Thus, to a higher band taxpayer, the £499.68 above will be reduced to £299.80.

Whether an individual GDP regards this as adequate recompense for the additional paperwork (which will be costly if it is processed by an accountant or some outside agency) and the risks of a dispute over the allowability of items, is a personal decision.

## Control visits

At intervals the GDP who registers as a VAT trader will be visited by a VAT Inspector, who will examine the records against the VAT returns to ensure the correct amounts are reclaimed. It is then that any discrepancies would become apparent and the trader could be called upon to repay any VAT wrongly repaid. Whether or not penalties would arise depends on individual circumstances. Control visits, as with the completion of the returns, does involve the GDP in time away from more profitable dental work.

## Deregistration

A GDP can, of course, deregister at any time after 12 months in the system, but it is then that an arbitrary value is put on any stocks or equipment held and the VAT will be payable. The situation could therefore arise, in which VAT repaid is due to be returned to the VAT authorities. It is a fallacy to believe that once VAT has been repaid on equipment, the GDP can deregister without paying back anything.

## Sale of the practice

On sale of the practice, it would seem that the sale value of the equipment will also be liable to VAT because it is disposal of a VATable item, if VAT has been reclaimed on it.

# 24

# Laboratories

Although the majority of GDPs will subcontract work on prosthetics to an outside contractor who is independent of the practice, there are still many who maintain an 'in-house facility'. The reasons for this is that the GDP will often perceive benefits, although these are perhaps more theoretical than real:

1   The GDP will retain control over how the technician works, the materials used and the priority given to various jobs. In reality it is rare for a GDP to have sufficient work to keep a technician fully employed, and much time may be wasted. In any event, a really busy GDP will not have the time or expertise to waste on such tasks.
2   The laboratory will usefully deploy space that would otherwise be wasted (eg a cellar). This may be true but the introduction of child education units run by an hygienist are likely to be more profitable in fee income and will certainly involve rather less capital investment. An average laboratory will require an outlay in equipment (benches, cabinets, furnaces, etc.) of around £15,000 which is about the same as a dental surgery. In addition there will be a stockholding in the order of £200 to £3000.
3   The availability of an 'in-house' technician will give a better service to patients, with speedy denture repairs, someone on hand to ease a denture or to make minor alterations to prosthetics, an opportunity to make colour matches, etc. It is, however, very wasteful for a technician to be called away from routine work to make minor adjustments that could easily be undertaken by the GDP. Even where a major alteration or a denture repair is necessitated, this can often by completed and returned in a couple of days.
4   There is an opportunity to make profit by taking in work from other practitioners in the area. However, other GDPs are not usually likely to use a laboratory owned and run by a colleague, partly because they would not necessarily wish them to see their models and partly because there is a resentment at allowing a colleague to make a profit from one's patients, albeit indirectly.

5. There are two distinct disadvantages:
   (a) Unless clearly separate records are maintained, including an internal billing of the practice and its associates, it will not be possible to know if the venture is profitable, and disputes with associates may be increased.
   (b) Prosthetic work is wide ranging and highly specialized. It is difficult to find a single technician who will be good at all aspects of the trade. Porcelain, gold or cobalt work may have to be subcontracted elsewhere, which will in some ways outweigh any advantages.

## Costings

Assuming that an 'in-house' laboratory is established and that the GDP is able to set up carefully maintained accounting records to demonstrate the operating results independently of the practice, the following percentages of the sale price are the targets:

| | |
|---|---|
| Materials | 17% |
| Labour | 46% |
| Overheads | 29% |
| Net pre-tax profit | 8% |
| | 100% |

The profit has, of course, to cover the capital investment, either interest on borrowed capital or 'opportunity cost', which is the loss of interest sustained through using money that might otherwise be used for a different purpose. This means a 'turnover' of at least £26,000 to break even.

The accounts of an independent laboratory will usually show a slightly better result than an 'in-house' one because there is no work interruption and the technician can keep up with work from other laboratories. There will also be no waste of resources by technicians trying to cope with work in which they are not especially skilled. Even so, the accounts of an independent laboratory do not reveal startling results, particularly if adjustment is made for the technician's own remuneration.

Profit and loss acount for the year ended 31 July 1992

| 1991 | | 1992 | 1992 |
|---|---|---|---|
| £ | | £ | £ |
| 54,330 | Income received | | 62,364 |
| 7,121 | Purchases | | 9,478 |
| 47,209 | Gross profit | | 52,886 |
| 66 | Staff wages | 4,107 | |
| 2,170 | Spouse's salary | 2,460 | |
| 316 | Rates and water | 872 | |
| 292 | Heating and lighting | 94 | |
| 514 | Insurance | 943 | |
| 431 | Repairs and renewals | 480 | |
| 159 | Telephone, printing and stationery | 149 | |
| 176 | Postage | 67 | |
| 3,620 | Motor and travelling expenses | | |
| | Petrol and oil | 1,048 | |
| | Repairs and maintenance | 1,038 | |
| | Licence and insurance | 322 | |
| | Tolls and car parking | 253 | |
| 1,215 | Accountancy | 1,350 | |
| 175 | Legal and professional | 50 | |
| – | Bank charges | 281 | |
| 1,130 | Bank interest | – | |
| 1,786 | Loan interest | 2,091 | |
| 639 | Hire purchase charges | 639 | |
| – | Subscriptions | 185 | |
| – | Cleaning | 70 | |

| £ | | £ | £ |
|---|---|---|---|
| – | Staff canteen | 101 | |
| – | Equipment maintenance | 824 | |
| – | Christmas festivities | 170 | |
| 690 | Sundry expenses | – | |
| 2,512 | Depreciation | 5,903 | |
| 15,891 | | | 22,522 |
| 31,318 | Net profit | | 29,389 |

# 25

# The accountant, the solicitor and collecting debts

GDPs will usually find that, in the course of their professional career they will need the help of various advisers. The bank manager has been dealt with in Chapter 7 and the insurance broker in Chapter 8. We now come to probably the most important advisers - the accountant and the solicitor.

## Accountant

There are four questions the dentist will ask when considering whether to instruct an accountant:

1   Do I really need one?
2   What can I expect of them?
3   What will their services cost?
4   Where do I find a good accountant?

### Do I really need an accountant?

It is not essential for any businessman to have an accountant because anyone can prepare their own accounts and negotiate with HMIT. However, it is unlikely that a busy GDP will have either the time or inclination to acquire the skills necessary to produce annual accounts accurately or to cope with the complexity of tax legislation. Indeed, their time is probably better and more profitably spent on clinical matters, for which they have been trained to a high standard, rather than trying to unravel complex tax regulations. There is also the point that HMIT is perhaps more likely to look closely at accounts prepared by the taxpayer in person, and certainly will have the advantage over the GDP in any tax negotiations. Furthermore, banks and other lending establishments are more likely to accept the accounts prepared by a properly trained individual, as will any potential partner or purchaser of the practice.

What can I expect of an accountant?

Apart from preparing annual accounts and negotiating with HMIT the accountant will probably be prepared to offer guidance on:

1   The strengths and weaknesses of the practice and how these can be rectified. If the accountant specializes in dental accounts they should have access to national averages and other specialist data.
2   When and how capital expenditure should be best incurred to achieve the most tax-efficient results.
3   The terms for engaging an associate or bringing in an expense-sharing colleague.
4   The value of goodwill for the purposes of a full or partial sale and, of course, the capital gains tax consequences of a particular course.
5   Investment of surplus funds.
6   Expansion or retraction of a practice, or its merger with another.
7   Pension plans.
8   Other business projects.
9   Other financial matters, including negotiation with the practice bankers for finance.
10   Raising funds in the best manner for tax purposes.
11   Estate planning.

There are, of course, a whole range of other services about which a properly trained accountant will have a wealth of experience and technical knowledge.


# How much will an accountant cost?

All accountants calculate their fees on the basis of time engaged, level of staff working on the task and the complexity of the job.

Quite clearly a GDP who maintains a good set of accounting records will doubtless find their accountancy fees very much less than one who simply throws everything in a box and leaves the accountant to sort out the muddle. Unfortunately, the greater majority of dentists fall into this category - their clinical records are probably very good but the accounts leave a great deal to be desired, with missing bank statements, blank cheque counterfoils, a dearth of invoices and probably no petty cash records. It is a waste of the accountant's time and the GDP's money to pay professional fees for the accountant to do the work of a book-keeper. Inevitably the larger accountancy firms will have higher hourly rates but can often offer a full range of services 'in house' whereas the sole practitioner may have to seek assistance from a colleague when problems arise. The smaller practice may offer a more personal service for a lower fee. It does not necessarily follow that the larger firms are better or the small ones are inferior.

# How do I find a good accountant?

This question is about as difficult as 'where do I find a good dentist?' Small firms can offer a more personal service with fewer changes of individual members of staff involved; larger firms may be able to provide a wider range of services and publications, although most sole practitioners have forged links with colleagues to fill any gap in the services that they offer in their own practices.

The GDP should approach a number of accountants and make a decision as to whom to instruct by considering the following points:

1   Is the accountant properly qualified and are their staff competent? Unlike dentistry, anyone can set up as an accountant (and many people do so and charge cut-rate fees); such people may have questionable ability or knowledge. Further, such individuals are often not insured against claims for professional negligence and it follows that if they make mistakes the GDP will have no redress. A Chartered or Certified Accountant has undergone specialist training and has passed relevant examinations. They will be subject to the disciplinary rules of their professional association, which will only issue a practising certificate on proof of adequate professional indemnity insurance. A registered auditor will  be licensed to undertake a company audit, which is evidence of acceptability to the Department of Trade.
2   Does the accountant have other dentist clients? The accounts and tax problems of a GDP have certain peculiarities, which are obviously better handled by someone with experience and skill in this field. It will be even better if the accountant has access to interpractice comparison data, which enables them to offer specialist advice.
3   What is the accountant's reputation with the Inland Revenue? Some accountants are popular with the Inland Revenue because they will readily concede any contentious point; others are exceedingly unpopular because they stand firm at all times. What is needed is an accountant who has a reputation for honesty but firmness in the face of a dispute.
4   How efficient is the accountant in dealing with correspondence and telephone calls, especially when the GDP is in urgent need of help?
5   Is the accountant willing to spend time with clients, ensuring that they understand the reasons for any advice and actions?

6    Does the accountant offer the full range of services that the GDP needs, and do they have access to help in the event of any problems?
7    Has the accountant given any indication of a desire to become acquainted with the GDP's professional and domestic problems.

It must, of course, be remembered that an accountant can only act within the constraint of information given by the GDP. The accounts prepared will determine the tax payable and can affect other decisions. If the records are defective, the accountant's work will be materially affected.

Accountancy fees do tend to increase annually, but this reflects the cost of employing quality staff and coping with ever increasing legislation. No accountant will simply undertake work to run up fees and most will be prepared to discuss their charges before undertaking a task and will be content to render interim accounts.

It is unwise for a GDP to constantly change accountant because this will suggest to HMIT that something is amiss and will attract unwelcome attention in the form of an 'in-depth' enquiry. Nor is it really prudent for an associate to have the same accountant as the principal, as this could create difficulties in the event of a disagreement. Indeed, some practitioners feel that expense sharing practitioners ought to be advised independently for the same reason.

By far the best way of finding an accountant is the recommendation of a colleague, although bodies such as the BDA might be able to assist. Simply picking a name from Yellow Pages or the professional list of members is a potentially hazardous course.

## The solicitor

It is less likely that a GDP will have a continuous use for a solicitor, but nevertheless it is wise to establish a  relationship with a solicitor in the same way as with other professionals. The sort of problems that give rise for legal advice include:

1    Purchase of a practice (or an interest in one).
2    Disputes with an associate, a colleague or even with staff.
3    Accident claims.
4    Negligence claims (although members of the DPL or MDU will be directed to their lawyers).
5    Debt collecting.
6    Renewal of leases.
7    Will.

The choice of a solicitor is very much the same as with an accountant but specialist knowledge is more important in purchase of a dental practice for agreements with an associate or colleague.

# Debt collecting

Anyone providing services to the general public in return for a fee will run the risk of non-payment and there is no way, other than payment in advance, that this can be avoided. There are always some people who will agree on a fee and then renege on the arrangement either through choice or force of circumstances.

Where possible, the reception staff should be instructed to collect the fee before the patient leaves at the end of a course of treatment, and staff should be instructed that payment by cheque needs to be supported by a banker's card. Payments by Access, Visa, Mastercard or American Express do not present the same problems provided the receptionist ensures that it is valid and not on the 'stop list'. However, if a patient does not pay at the time and requests for settlement are continuously ignored, the matter can be placed in the hands of a debt collector, who usually work on a no-return-no-fee basis, or, in the last resort, by a summons through the Small Claims Court.

## The small claims court

This involves completing a form and taking it with a copy of the bill and a cheque for the Court fee to the local County Court Office. The Court will issue the summons and, if there is no response within fourteen days judgement will be entered. If a defence is filed the Court will fix a date for a pre-trial review, which is a fairly informal meeting by both parties with the Registrar to decide whether there is a case to go to arbitration. If there is, a date is fixed and both parties are heard before the Registrar (now known as the District Judge) who gives an award which, other than on points of law, is binding on everyone.

If a defence is filed the case is transferred to a Court near to the defendant's home or business. This means that the case will be heard there and, as this could involve not only time off work but also costly travelling it may be questionable as to whether the claim is worth pursuing. Costs are not awarded, which means that the plaintiff could still be out of pocket even if successful.

Unfortunately, far too many people will pursue a claim as a matter of principle but fail to realize that this could be more expensive than simply abandoning the issue.

# Other arbitrations

It may be worthwhile bearing in mind that many disputes can be resolved by arbitration, including those between principal and associate. This is often a straightforward way to settle an argument, and will almost certainly be less expensive than litigation.

# 26

# Inland Revenue investigations

In 1976 the Inland Revenue announced that it intended to simplify the work of HMIT by passing accounts with a cursory examination only, but that some cases would be selected for an 'in-depth' examination. Whilst the original intention was to select such cases randomly, this was found to be impracticable because the work load imposed by cases which clearly demanded investigation was heavy. The rate of investigations, particularly amongst dentists, has increased sharply in recent years and it does seem that there is a measure of random selection, although this has been denied. It is claimed that cases are chosen only for good reasons, but in some instances the justification put forward is tenuous. The fact is that investigatory work has released substantial sums in tax interest and penalties – in a few instances simply to achieve settlement – however, the poor quality of accounting records maintained by the average GDP has certainly contributed to this success rate.

## Reasons for investigation

Amongst the reasons given by HMIT for instigating an enquiry are the following:

1   An erratic pattern of expenses against fee income as compared with national averages, although sometimes it is clear that HMIT does not understand dental accounts.
2   An erratic pattern of drawings and personal expenditure, which suggests that there might be some other source of income or suppression of fees.
3   Failure to notify chargeability to tax within the statutory time limit.
4   Consistent late filing of accounts or tax returns.
5   An obvious omission from a tax return.

## Commencement of an enquiry

The first indication of a pending investigation is usually a letter from HMIT asking very searching questions about accounts, which, to an experienced accountant, will show the direction of thought by the Inspector. This may well be followed by a request for sight of the original accounting records, business and personal bank statements, building society pass books and other items.

The immediate reaction of most GDPs will be that they have nothing to hide, which may well be the case. As a result, the GDP may ask the accountant to seek to dissuade the Inspector from pursuing matters, but this would be an exceedingly unwise move. If there is nothing to cause concern, there is clearly no reason to refuse to co-operate. Any attempt to divert HMIT from a chosen course will simply arouse more suspicion. Probably the best approach is first to ask whether a formal 'in-depth' enquiry is being commenced and the reasons for this (whether or not the response will be entirely frank will depend upon the circumstances, but it is likely to evoke a generalized or vague response, which may point to a random selection).

The sensible course would be to produce the accounting records, more especially as the HMIT, who has a duty to be satisfied with the accuracy of the accounts, is entitled to see them.

Problems may arise if the records sought include the names or any other confidential information about patients and their treatment. The GDP should remember that such data will appear not only on the clinical record cards but also on the supporting pages to the DPB Schedules, detailed technicians' invoices and even in the appointment book. The relationship between GDP and patients is confidential and, if this is breached for any reason without the patient's consent, it is likely that the dentist could face disciplinary proceedings before the GDC.

HMIT will probably claim to be bound by the Official Secrets Act. This is irrelevant because once the information leaves the practice, the GDP has no control over its use – it may be used to assist HMIT in pursuing separate enquiries into the affairs of the patient. HMIT may also point out that they could seek a production order under Section 20 ITMA (1970) but the response to this should be that it will be opposed and, if necessary, taken to the Court of Appeal. It is unlikely (especially as the contents are not likely to be of much value) that the Inspector will pursue matters further by embarking upon a confrontation. The request may very well be dropped. The support schedules to the DPB statements will certainly serve no purpose because the data is summarized on the front sheet; the appointment book will disclose little because it is unlikely to show the appointment failures.

Throughout, the GDP should be frank and honest with the Inspector. If the GDP has diverted funds or concealed any income this should be disclosed promptly because it will be in the best interests of the taxpayer in the end. The GDP's co-operation will be an important factor in the assessment of penalties and consequently it is not sensible to be unnecessarily obstructive.

The Inland Revenue will expect proof of the source of all income that is claimed to be non-taxable. Where such proof is not forthcoming, it is most likely that the Inspector will seek to treat the money as diverted fees chargeable to tax.

## Interview

Having carried out a review of the accounting records, HMIT will doubtless have a number of questions and an interview will be sought with the GDP to discuss matters. A prudent accountant will suggest that, whilst a meeting is not opposed in principle, it would be sensible to clear most issues through correspondence, because a meeting would otherwise waste the GDP's valuable time. Doubtless HMIT will think otherwise, but it is worth remembering that HMIT may be looking at the interview as a 'fishing expedition' to see what information can be gathered to further enquiries. This objective is more difficult to achieve in correspondence, which affords the GDP and any advisers time to consider the implications of any questions raised.

If and when a meeting is agreed, the Inspector should be asked to produce an agenda in advance. He will be reluctant to do so but will if pressed sufficiently. The value of the agenda is that it will not only keep the meeting brief and to the point but will give a better idea of where matters are leading and enable the accountant and GDP to plan accordingly. It is also desirable that the meeting should take place in the accountant's office, which will clearly be less intimidating for the taxpayer and will put HMIT at a disadvantage. Every effort should be made to refuse to have the meeting at the dental practice or the GDP's home.

The accountant should be present throughout the meeting and should make notes, intervening only when necessary to clarify a question or to suggest that a particular matter be left unanswered until a later date in correspondence; the accountant should be ready to bring the meeting to a close if necessary. The GDP should keep all answers brief and to the point - all too often a taxpayer is so nervous that they will wander off the point and talk far too much, accidentally volunteering other lines of enquiry to the Inspector. Odd comments made during the interview or even in the relaxed closing stages when it seems HMIT has concluded matters can be exceedingly damaging.

The accountant may be asked by HMIT for a copy of the notes but it is not sensible to accede to this request – it is not for the taxpayer to provide evidence to be used against himself.

## Concluding stages

After the meeting has been held or, where the accountant or GDP decline to meet the Inspector and correspondence has exhausted matters, HMIT will put forward proposals indicating the amount of tax and interest considered to have been lost. The GDP will be asked to sign a Certificate of Disclosure and a Statement of Assets and Liabilities. The former is regarded as essential to demonstrate that everything has been disclosed, and will be the basis for a possible prosecution if it proves subsequently to be incorrect. The latter is to get firmly in writing from the taxpayer precisely what assets they have at a particular point in time, again a useful aid if the enquiries are reopened later.

Sometimes either the taxpayer or accountant is inclined to accept what HMIT says about interest and culpability; but this ought to be examined carefully because there have been many instances in which an over-zealous official has been mistaken and has sought penalties in cases where they are not appropriate. An offer is then invited to embrace the tax, interest and penalties.

Once an offer has been made, accepted and the tax paid, the investigation is at an end. An enquiry seldom ends up in criminal proceedings, although where the Enquiry or Special Branches are involved it is a distinct possibility.

It is unlikely that the taxpayer will be hounded once an enquiry is at an end, but there are cases in which the exercise is repeated because further circumstances suggest that either the original cases was not properly concluded or that the taxpayer has continued upon a course of tax evasion.

## Penalties

Inevitably there are penalties for tax misdemeanours – prosecution is usual only in very exceptional circumstances but almost certainly where deliberate fraud is involved. The penalties are usually of a pecuniary nature:

1   Failure to notify chargeability to tax: £300
2   Failure to submit an income tax return: £50
    If after the penalty is imposed the default continues, there is an additional penalty of £60 per day during the period of default.

3   Tax lost through negligence or fraud – 100% of the tax mitigated by
    the following percentages

(a)   full disclosure:          30%

(b)   full co-operation:        40%

(c)   gravity:                  40%

                           —————

                          110%

Every accountant is aware that investigations are not confined to the practice accounts. Sometimes the enquiry relates to the payroll and is conducted by the Wages Audit staff from the office of the Collector of Taxes. These are directed at cases where the tax has not been properly deducted from wages or other staff benefits, and they too can culminate in a demand for tax, interest and penalties.

There are penalties for failure to correctly operate a PAYE scheme or to submit the Employer's Annual Return (form P35) but these do not normally involve a full-scale 'in-depth' enquiry.

Where penalties are involved, there are frequently informal discussions between the accountant and HMIT to establish the sort of penalty that would be acceptable.

# The offer

Once the offer is made in writing and accepted there is a binding contract, which can be enforced through the Courts if necessary. Payment is usually expected within 30 days of acceptance and, if it is the intention of the GDP to seek to make an instalment offer, this must be made clear at the time the written offer is submitted.

# Legal responsibility

Very occasionally a taxpayer will blame failure to deal with returns and accounts expeditiously on their accountant; this is no answer so far as the Inland Revenue is concerned. The accountant is legally an agent of the taxpayer and it is the GDP who is responsible for both the submission and accuracy of the tax returns and accounts, as well as for compliance with time limits.

## Taxpayer's charter

The Inland Revenue has now produced what it terms the 'Taxpayer's Charter', which provides as follows:

> You are entitled to expect the Inland Revenue:
> (a) to be fair:
>   (i)    by settling your tax affairs impartially
>   (ii)   by expecting you to pay only what is due under the law
>   (iii)  by treating everyone with equal fairness
> (b) to help you:
>   (i)    to get your tax affairs right
>   (ii)   to understand your rights and obligations
>   (iii)  by providing clear leaflets and forms
>   (iv)   by giving you information and assistance at their enquiry offices
>   (v)    by being courteous at all times
> (c) to provide an efficient service:
>   (i)    by settling your tax affairs promptly and accurately
>   (ii)   by keeping your private affairs strictly confidential
>   (iii)  by using the information you give only as allowed by the law
>   (iv)   by keeping to a minimum your costs of complying with the law
>   (v)    by keeping their costs down
> (d) to be accountable for what they do by setting standards themselves and publishing how well they live up to them.

If you are not satisfied:

(a) The Inland Revenue will tell you exactly how to complain
(b) You can ask for your tax affairs to be looked at again
(c) You can appeal to an independent tribunal
(d) Your MP can refer your complaint to the Ombudsman.

In return, the Inland Revenue needs you to:

(a) Be honest
(b) Give accurate information
(c) Pay your tax on time.

# General

There is no certain way to avoid an investigation and all anyone can do is to take precautions:

1   Notification of liability should be made within the statutory time limit.
2   All income tax returns should be carefully completed and submitted promptly.
3   Accounts should be produced as soon as possible after the close of the financial year and care should be taken to ensure they are accurate, and in particular that the work in progress and debtors are accurate, drawings are adequate and any unusual fluctuation in expenditure, etc. is properly explained.
4   The basic accounting records are completed and accurate and agree with the final accounts. Attention should be paid to the careful and accurate recording of all cash income and expenditure. The system outlined in this book would be adequate if properly maintained.
5   A careful record should be maintained as to the source of monies paid into private bank accounts, building society accounts, etc. for the dentist, their spouse and minor children. Any supporting evidence should be retained because it is difficult to remember the source of any particular sum after a number of years.
6   The golden rule is to destroy nothing but to ensure that all paperwork is readily accessible and complete.

# 27

# Insolvency

It is often said that many dentists live beyond their incomes; this may be due to a number of factors. Often it is due to an extravagant lifestyle. Sometimes it is because mortgages, life assurance and pension schemes have over-stretched the dentist's finances. In a few cases it is due to the collapse of a business into which the GDP has ventured as a 'side-line', oblivious of the fact that dentists are not known generally for their business acumen.

All too often the accountant gives warnings of drawings exceeding profit and the inevitable consequences. GDPs who do not heed such predictions have no-one but themselves to blame for the threatening letters, writs, bailiff visits and ultimate arrival of the bankruptcy notice. It is sometimes too late to take adequate remedial action when the dentist finally awakens to their predicament.

A practitioner who is warned of impending disaster should seek to put matters right rather than seek some cosmetic solution such as borrowing further money or seeking to release the equity in their home or surgery. It is a good idea to go to the root of the problem and seek either to increase their earnings or to severely restrict personal expenditure, even to the extent of putting some life assurance or pension policies 'on ice' until matters improve materially. Sadly, few are prepared to take such steps and prefer the Micawber-style approach.

GDPs who are faced with an impossible position should discuss the situation with an Insolvency Practitioner, who is trained to handle such matters. It may be that the GDP should consider a voluntary arrangement with creditors; the Insolvency Practitioner will be able to arrange this scheme.

As a last resort the GDP may have to accept bankruptcy as a solution. This may be achieved either by filing a petition or allowing a creditor to do this. The debtor will file their own petition at the local Bankruptcy Court by paying the appropriate fee.

A creditor can take the action by presenting the petition to the High Court, paying the fee and a deposit towards the costs of the Official Receiver in Bankruptcy.

Whether or not an outside trustee is appointed will depend upon the individual circumstances; if there are adequate assets this is most likely but, where there are none, it is probable that the Official Receiver will act in that capacity.

Initially the debtor will have an interview with the Official Receiver's examiner, who will enquire into the bankrupt's conduct and the reasons for the insolvency. Provided there is nothing serious amiss, it is likely that this will be an end to the matter, although the examiner may suggest a voluntary arrangement and put a proposal to the creditors.

The dentist is, of course, not prevented from practising once adjudicated bankrupt but they have the following disabilities during the period of bankruptcy (3 years):

1  They cannot have a bank account.
2  They must disclose their status on obtaining credit.
3  They risk the Official Receiver/Trustee seeking to take  part of their earnings for the creditors.
4  They risking the loss of any significant after-acquired property.

However, the GDP cannot be prevented from earning a living by following their profession, inevitably as an associate.

Until the late 1980s it was comparatively rare to find an insolvent dentist but today, regrettably, a large number face this situation as they continue to live beyond their incomes.

# 28

# Statistical data

It is comparatively easy for a GDP to compare the results of their practice one year with the next, provided they can eliminate the effects of inflation. It is not quite so easy to gain access to the means of checking whether the practice compares favourably with similar practices elsewhere, or whether it is as profitable as it ought to be.

## Year-by-year comparison

The elimination of inflation in order to compare annual results shown in the accounts is achieved by multiplying last years figures by:

$$\frac{\text{This year's Retail Price Index}}{\text{Last year's Retail Price Index}}$$

This is a fairly crude method of converting last year's money into the equivalent purchasing power of this year's money. It does, nevertheless, give a fairly reasonable basis for comparison. The main problems are:

1 The Retail Price Index (RPI) covers the 'shopping basket' of commodities purchased by the average household but is not geared specifically to changes in the cost of dental supplies.
2 As expenditure is not consistent throughout the year it is probably best to take the RPI at mid-point in each financial year.

# Interpractice comparison

This is not easy to achieve because data is not readily available. Simply listening to colleagues is an unreliable method because no-one is likely to admit to being unsuccessful in practice. Industry and commerce have had the benefit for some years of the Centre for Interfirm Comparison, which collects anonymous data from individual companies, processes it and then produces comparative tables. It has a wide database, which means it can compare 'like with like' as regards size, location, structure and working environment. Unfortunately it has not included dentistry or dental laboratories in its surveys.

The Institute of Chartered Accountants has established a comparison scheme for accountants, which is up-dated on an annual basis. There has been some talk of a similar scheme in the dental world but as yet this has not come to fruition.

The only data currently available is that collected by CODE  (the Confederation of Dental Employers) and by individual accountants who specialize in dental practice accounting and have a large database of information available. Unfortunately this statistical information is retained for internal use and is available only to the clients of the practices concerned.

In 1976 an attempt was made in Kent to establish a scheme for comparisons, and a pilot survey was published in *Dental Update* in January 1977. However, GDPs were apprehensive about providing data, even anonymously, because of fear that it could fall into the hands of the Department of Health.

Hopefully at some stage in the future a suitable survey will be established to which any practitioner will be able  to subscribe.

# Software systems with DPB transmission certification

**Arthur**
Team Management Systems Ltd
Unit 4D Watlington Industrial Estate
Cuxham Road
Watlington
OX9 5LU

**Clockwork**
Broadland Distribution Ltd
Broadland House
53a South Park Road
Wimbledon
London
SW19 8RT

**SDS – Specialist Dental Services Ltd**
Westside House
123 Bath Row
Edgbaston
Birmingham
BH15 1LS

**SFD – Systems for Dentists**
90 High Street
Gosforth
Newcastle-Upon-Tyne
NE3 1HB

**Shire Dental System**
Shire Medical Software Ltd
Business Technology Centre
Radway Green Venture Park
Radway Green Road
Cheshire
CW2 5PR

**Star Status**
Status Point Ltd
9 Colne Way Court
Colne Way
Watford
WD2 4NE

**VAMP**
Value Added Medical Products Ltd
The Bread Factory
1a Broughton Street
London
SW8 3QJ

# Some useful addresses

British Dental Association
64 Wimpole Street
London
W1M 8AL

Dental Protection Ltd.
80 Great Portland Street
London
WC1E 5PA

Faculty of General Dental Practitioners
Royal College of Surgeons of England
35/43 Lincoln's Inn Fields
London
WC2A 3PN

General Dental Council
37 Wimpole Street
London
W1M 8DQ

Medical Defence Union
3 Devonshire Place
London
W1N 2EA

Medical Insurance Agency
Hertlands House
Primet Road
Stevenage
SG1 3EE

# Schedule D changes

In the 1993 Budget the Chancellor of the Exchequer announced changes in the basis of assessment under Schedule D, which are aimed at simplifying the system. With effect from 5 April, 1997 all assessments will be based on actual profit, as opposed to the preceding year basis. This means that 1995/96 will be the last year to be based on the complicated system currently in force. The fiscal year 1996/97 will be a transitional year. The Inland Revenue will, for that year alone, base the assessment on the average profit shown by:

1   The financial year ending between 6 April 1996 and 5 April 1997.
2   That of the previous accounting period.

Example: Profit for the year to 28 February:

1995: normally assessable 1995/96: £40,000

1996: normally assessable 1996/97: £50,000

1997: normally assessable 1997/98: £60,000

1998: normally assessable 1998/99: £70,000

Effect of change:

1995/96: existing rules: £30,000

1996/97: transitional year: average of £50,000 (i.e. year to 28 February 1996) and £60,000 (i.e. year to 28 February 1997): £55,000

1997/98: first year of new system: £60,000

It will be seen that the Inland Revenue will 'lose' one year, and it is sensible to keep the profits up for each of the two years ending 28 February 1996 and 1997 to ensure a higher average and consequently a greater loss to the Inland Revenue. This can be achieved either by expediting or deferring any non-essential revenue expenditure.

Thereafter our taxation system should be easier to understand and tax will be paid on actual profits made although, bearing in mind the dates of payment of tax and the charge for interest, it will be prudent for dentists to ensure that their accounts are completed and submitted to the Inspector of Taxes promptly.

Example: Profit for the year to 28 February 1998 will be the basis for the year 1997/98. The tax will be payable by two equal instalments on 1 January 1998 (whilst the year is still in progress) and 1 July 1998 (just two months after the end of the tax year).

# Abbreviations

| | |
|---|---|
| BA | Balancing Allowance |
| BC | Balancing Charge |
| BDA | British Dental Association |
| BDJ | British Dental Journal |
| BPMF | British Postgraduate Medical Federation |
| BUPA | British United Provident Association |
| CGT | Capital Gains Tax |
| DPB | Dental Practice Board |
| DPS | Dental Protection Society |
| DSA | Dental Surgery Assistant |
| DSS | Department of Social Security |
| FHSA | Family Health Services Authority |
| GDC | General Dental Council |
| GDP | General Dental Practitioner |
| GDS | General Dental Services |
| HMCO | Her Majesty's Collector of Taxes |
| HMIT | Her Majesty's Inspector of Taxes |
| IR | Inland Revenue |
| MDU | Medical Defense Union |
| NHS | National Health Service |
| NI | National Insurance |
| NIC | National Insurance Contributions |
| PAYE | Pay As You Earn |
| PPP | Private Patients Plan |

| RPI | Retail Price Index |
| SMP | Statutory Maternity Pay |
| SSP | Statutory Sick Pay |
| TAGI | Target Average Gross Income |
| TANI | Target Average Net Income |
| VAT | Value Added Tax |
| VT | Vocational Trainee |
| WDA | Written Down Allowance |
| WDV | Written Down Value |

# Dental Health Schemes

The following companies may be contacted for further information on dental health schemes currently available.

Bristol Contributory Welfare
Association Ltd
Bristol House
40–56 Victoria St
Bristol
BS1 6AB

BUPA Central Publicity
Provident House
Essex Street
London
WC2R 3AX

BUPA Dental Cover
Heron House
Sixth Floor
8–10 Christchurch Road
Bournemouth
BH1 3NP

CDC
Westbourne House
115 Station Road
Hayes
Middlesex
UB3 4BX

CIGNA
Tower House
38 Trinity Square
London
EC3N 4DJ

Denplan
Denplan Court
Victoria Road
Winchester
Hampshire
SO23 7RG

Densure plc
8 Caxton Hill
Hertford
SG13 7NE

Dentoplan
Overseas House
19–23 Ironmonger Row
London
EC1V 3QN

Direct Debit Services Ltd
5 Salcott Crescent
New Addington
Surrey
CRO 0JG

Hospital Savings Association
Hambledon House
Andover
Hampshire
SP10 1LQ

Mida Dental Plans
Pinnacle House
23–26 St Dunstans Hill
London
EC3R 8HL

National Dental Plan
Ibex House
Minories
London
EC3N 1DY

Norwich Union Healthcare
Chilworth House
Templars Way
Hampshire Corporate Park
Eastleigh
Hampshire
SO5 3RY

Optimedia
84–86 Baker Street
London
W1A 1DL

Smile Dental Plan
Imperium
Imperial Way
Reading
Berkshire
RG2 0UD

Status Point Ltd
9 Colne Way Court
Colne Way
Watford
Hertfordshire
WD2 4NE

Alexander Stenhouse UK Ltd
230 High Street
Potters Bar
Hertfordshire
EN6 5BU

Strasbourgeoise
90 Sloane Street
London
SW1X 9PQ

Unity Healthcare
40 Fountain Street
Manchester
M2 2AB

WPA
Rivergate House
Blackbrook Park
Taunton
Somerset
TA1 2PE

# INDEX

For Product Safety Concerns and Information please contact our EU
representative GPSR@taylorandfrancis.com
Taylor & Francis Verlag GmbH, Kaufingerstraße 24, 80331 München, Germany